ALSO BY E. L. DOCTOROW

Welcome to Hard Times

Big as Life

The Book of Daniel

Ragtime

Drinks Before Dinner (play)

Loon Lake

Lives of the Poets

World's Fair

Billy Bathgate

Jack London, Hemingway, and the Constitution

JACK LONDON, HEMINGWAY, AND THE CONSTITUTION

Selected Essays, 1977–1992

E. L. DOCTOROW

RANDOM HOUSE

NEW YORK

Portions of this book have been previously published in *Architectural Digest, Gettysburg Review, Harper's Magazine, The Michigan Quarterly Review, The Nation, New American Review, Playboy,* and *The New York Times Book Review.*

"Two Waldens" was originally published in *Heaven Is Under Our Feet,* edited by Dawn Henly and David Marsh (Longmeadow Press, 1991).

". . . and His Call of the Wild" was originally published as the introduction to the Library of America edition of *The Call of the Wild* (Vintage Books, 1990).

Grateful acknowledgment is made to Bantam Books, a division of the Bantam, Doubleday, Dell Publishing Group, Inc., for permission to reprint the introduction by E. L. Doctorow to *Sister Carrie* by Theodore Dreiser (Bantam Books, 1982). Reprinted by permission.

Library of Congress Cataloging-in-Publication Data

Doctorow, E. L.

Jack London, Hemingway, and the Constitution: selected essays, 1977–1992 / E. L. Doctorow. — 1st ed.

p.   cm.

ISBN 0-679-42686-8

I. Title.

PS3554.O3J33   1993   814'.54—dc20   93-4179

Manufactured in the United States of America

Designed by J. K. Lambert

2 3 4 5 6 7 8 9

First Edition

ACKNOWLEDGMENTS

I am indebted to Sam Cohn for insisting on this book . . .

. . . and to my assistants Nathaniel Penn and Jane Malmo, who recovered the original texts and put together a manuscript I could work from . . .

. . . and to Helen Henslee for her fondness for the work of Jack London and Ernest Hemingway, and her high regard for the Constitution of the United States.

Introduction

With one exception the pieces in this book were written because someone asked me to write them. Left to my own devices I will write fiction. I will choose the thrown voice and all its tropes. But when invited to write in my own voice for occasions not of my own devising, now and then, for one good or ignoble reason or another, I will do that.

The earliest of the pieces was written in 1977, the most recent in 1992. I'm surprised to find that they have in common a kind of presumptive nationalism. They seem to concern themselves with American texts—printed or otherwise ingrained, those we recognize as ours and those we don't. I've set them in what I hope is, roughly, the order of a thought process that goes: from the lives of some classic American authors, to the place of their work in the composition of our national character, to the ideas we can take from them as applicable to ourselves and our times, to our times as they're constructed by our politics, to the states of mind we live in that we call our culture.

I can't be sure that another selection in another order wouldn't reveal the same underlying presumption. The writers I speak of (white male) made of themselves repositories of American myth, and the presidents I speak of (also white male) held mythic values no less vaunting. Ultimately, what politicians do becomes another kind of writing—perhaps like Kafka's harrow, working its needles into the skin. But there is a real continuum insofar as those who make history write it, just as those who write it make it, an idea I give its fullest expression in the essay "False Documents," and also acknowledge in a reflection on George Orwell's mythbook, *1984*, a superstatist American text, for all its nightmare European imagery.

But there is no text more central to our lives than our Constitution, which I treat here as Scripture, meaning a text that is read and studied and interpreted with statutory law, just as the scripture of Judaism, Christianity, or Islam is read and studied and interpreted.

And finally, as to American texts, there is the text of our cheapened dreams, our culture of popular song, the *standards*, as we call them, that sing in our heads generation after generation as a sort of urtext of the collective unconscious.

Where writers are not locked in history is Heaven, eventless Heaven. For all the variety of their subjects, these essays are necessarily spoken from the cultural milieu of the late, long cold war, which, one way or another, framed American intellectual life for almost half a century. I was a high school student in 1946 when Winston Churchill made his Iron Curtain speech at Fulton, Missouri. I published my first novel the year John F. Kennedy was elected president. Not that I'm alone—almost all the writers publishing today came up in the cold war. In fact, just how long the war lasted may be realized by considering that, as to our literature, only one generation is still alive—writers in or verging on their seventies—whose working life has not been entirely circumscribed by it.

With the fall of the Berlin Wall in 1989, and the breakdown of the Soviet Union, the war was declared over, but without any corresponding national sense of elation. If I were giving a State of the Mind of the Union address, I would describe us today as convalescing. "Reality outraces apprehension," Melville says, speaking of the white whale, and so in spirit, in body, we are still to some extent suffering our cold war. This may have to do with the years of our denial. There were times when we were so inured to the war's dangers that we lived and worked as if it didn't exist. Children were born, went to school, married, and had children. Careers were embarked upon, the rhythms of private life tolled off the years. Yet the cold war was a fifty-year nuclear alert with two full-fledged nonnuclear clashes, Korea and Vietnam, fought in its shadow, and innumerable surrogate wars, covert subversions of foreign governments, coups, incursions, skirmishes, forays, international incidents, and nuclear weapons tests performed in its service. What is more, though the enemy to be contained was the Soviet Union, the creative animus of our warring mind was unleashed, to an astonishing degree, upon ourselves.

The penultimate piece in this book, "James Wright at Kenyon," recalls the poet, my friend, during our undergraduate days in the American darkness of the late forties and early fifties. *Time* was to call us "the silent generation"—as who, under the circumstances, would not be? An ideology of fear, sincerely or cynically broadcast by the politicians of the moment, devolved into a powerful civil religion with distinctly Puritan cruelties. Absolutist and Manichaean, it discovered and purged the designated subversive elements among us, not only with legal prosecutions where crimes had been committed, but with sworn oaths of loyalty, blacklists, and public rituals of confession and repentance before congressional committees where no crimes were supposed to have occurred other than crimes of thought.

That was the cold war's first phase. In its second phase, during the sixties, it took the lives of over fifty thousand of our young, and wounded and maimed tens of thousands more. Vietnam was the cold war's most absurd expression and attenuated rationale, and provoked a generation of students to arise in dissent and massively challenge its rigid orthodoxies. Their dissidence had the dynamic of a Reformation, the young rising against their elders' dogma and its attendant culture and proposing another. At no other time since the Civil War has the country been so grievously torn.

In the aftermath of Vietnam, the generational survivors of the fifty thousand dead found themselves once again in an America unfazed, a land of pod people, the children behind them coming out studious, obedient, and smelling as clean as new car models. This was the third phase, akin to Counter-Reformation—the Right's chastisement of the ungrateful known as Morning in America.

In this final decade or so, with the mandate of a populace compliant with ruling circumstances, the last administrations of the cold war conflated its ideology with the capitalist principles of the nineteenth century. Deregulating industry, dismantling social legislation of benefit to anyone but their core constituencies, abjuring law enforcement where the law was not to their liking, and politicizing the courts, they distributed the enormous costs of the cold war democratically among all the classes of society except the wealthiest. The effect on our national standard of living was as a vampire's arterial suck.

When the historians get to work they will have to consider the proposition that this half century of cold war generated as discrete a social and cultural pathology as any other of our wars. And that it constituted an act of national self-mutilation all the more astonishing for the greatness of the country that performed it.

So I publish these essays in an uncommonly distinct historical moment, when that era has ended, and another, still to be defined, has begun. How can any writer-citizen not bless himself for having outlasted the long cold decades of his time? How can he not pray for the dead and for the maligned and destitute . . . and not offer whatever documents he has to the communal articulation of the new era and the national future we hope to find for ourselves?

New York
March 1993

Contents

JACK LONDON AND HIS CALL OF THE WILD

Jack London . . .

The most comprehensive collection of Jack London's letters, over fifteen hundred of them, fills three volumes in the voice of the phenomenal sire of Buck and White Fang, Wolf Larsen and Martin Eden, from his days as the Boy Socialist of Oakland and youthful Klondike backpacker to the eve of his death at forty, of uremia, or stroke, or accidental overdose of his painkiller of preference, heroin, or perhaps all of these, but really of exhaustion, of having lived so as to feel every moment of his life to the limit, and to see the cruelly farcical conclusion to so many of his dreams.

He grew up in and around Oakland, California. His mother was Flora Wellman, a cold, bitter little woman given to spiritualism. His father of record, John London, was a failed storekeeper who worked at the end of his life as a night watchman on the Oakland docks. The family's shameful secret was that Jack's real father was William Chaney, an itinerant astrologer and all-around con man who had lived with Flora Wellman out of wedlock and abandoned her when she became pregnant. When his son finally learned this and wrote to him, Chaney denied his paternity. This was about the time the young man's favorite author, Rudyard Kipling, published *The Jungle Book*, with its tale of Mowgli, a human child raised by wolves to live the honorably savage ways of the wild. Jack London symbolized himself as a kind of feral orphan all his life.

The author's teenage years were conditioned by the economic depressions of the times. He worked long hours in a cannery and a jute mill. Scrappy and in a hurry to grow up, he learned the habit of manly drinking in saloons on the Oakland waterfront. He turned himself into an expert small-boat sailor and used a little skiff to loot the commercial oyster beds of the South Bay. At seventeen he shipped out as an able-bodied seaman on a sealing schooner to Japan, the Bokin Islands, and the Bering Sea. On his return he shoveled coal ten hours a day for the Oakland, San Leandro, and Hayward Electric Railway. Then he hit the road again, this time joining the western contingent of Coxey's Army, a march of the unemployed upon Washington, but quitting by the time he got to Missouri and wandering on his own as far as Buffalo, where he was arrested for vagrancy and served a thirty-day jail sentence that probably included sexual abuse at the hands of the inmates.

Returning home, he vowed to raise himself out of the poverty, menial labor, and social degradation he named "The Pit." From his early childhood he had been a reader: fiction, philosophy, poetry, political theory—everything. Now he saw in books the means to his freedom. He joined a debating society and found friends in the community of local Socialists. He was a sturdy, handsome blond fellow with wide-set blue eyes, a square jaw, and a great intensity of feeling that people found charismatic. His best friends were Ted and Mabel Applegarth, brother and sister, a cut or two above him in education and dress and manners. He learned some of the softer ways of gentility from them, and began to court Mabel.

The young man became a popular speaker for the Socialist Labor Party. He had read Marx and concluded that the terrors of the life of the lower classes could not be eliminated by anything less than a revolution in the American economic system. His letters to the editor were published in the papers. A fair example of his political self-confidence is to be found in a letter dated 1896, when, age twenty, he writes to the *Oakland Times* to warn of the illusory value of competition between the two Oakland water companies: "Selling water at a loss, the company with the smallest capital . . . will go under. The other company will now . . . make Oaklanders who enjoyed the low rates sweat, by raising them. . . . Competition [is] a waste of labor and capital, and always results in monopoly. Is there any path out of the wilderness? . . . I would ask [the reader] if he has ever heard of municipal ownership?" This sort of thing brought him notoriety as the "Boy Socialist of Oakland." But he was not really precocious; he had lived in his twenty years enough to have gained the experience, and with it the self-assurance, of a man twice his age. The genius of his life, and its torment, finally, was its accelerated rate.

There is something else: He was a quick study and leapt on the history of his times like a man to the back of a horse. When the gold fever came to San Francisco, Socialist or not, he caught it and joined the rush to the Klondike to find his fortune.

Of course he would join the gold rush. It was the hardy test of manhood and promise of wealth that no red-blooded American socialist could resist. "I expect to carry 100 lbs. to the load on good trail, and on the worst 75 lbs.," he wrote Mabel from Alaska in a tone of self-commiserating heroism. "For every mile . . . I will have to travel from 20 to 30 miles. I have 1000 lbs. in my outfit." Yet he must have had some hope or prevision of the Yukon as the land of his literary dreams. He made the difficult portage only to spend the winter snowbound in a cabin south of Dawson City. Then he developed scurvy, and rather than pan for gold, he convalesced in the saloons of Dawson and listened to the tales of the sourdoughs. Here was the large romance of cold, bitter life to suit his theories. By the spring of the following year, recovered partially from his scurvy and totally from his gold fever, he rafted down the Yukon River and returned by steamer to San Francisco with exactly four and a half dollars in gold dust for his effort.

But he came away with something that, as he himself said, enabled him to "pan out a living" for the rest of his life. He had found a country for his imagination, a terrain for his orphan soul.

Methodically setting himself the task of becoming a professional author, Jack analyzed the stories he liked, or copied them out by hand so as to learn how they were put together, and wrote his own pieces with their example in mind. He mailed so much stuff off to the magazines that he had to devise a system of record-keeping to keep track of it. Rejections poured in. But within a year he had sold a tale of the Northland to the *Atlantic Monthly* and he was off and running. He published his first collection of short stories, *The Son of the Wolf*, in 1900, and true to the rapid metabolism of his fate, four short years later he was the most popular writer in the country.

Industrial America turned out to have a vast appetite for the romance of Nature, for the adventure of creatures, human or animal, unmediated by civilization. By 1904 Jack London was the author of ten published books, including *The Call of the Wild*, *A Daughter of the Snows*, *Children of the Frost*, and his classic novel *The Sea Wolf*. His pieces, essays, and stories filled the magazines. He wrote from the capital of his emotionally desolate boyhood, and from the life he had seen on the sea and the land, and from the servitude he had endured. He wrote prodigious amounts. The big newspapers hired him out as foreign correspondent. In England on the way to cover the Boer War for the Associated Press he was called off the assignment and, making the most of his situation, dropped out of sight and became a denizen of the slums of London's East End, emerging to write *The People of the Abyss*, a classic of investigative reporting on poverty and homelessness, which he produced in seven weeks.

Jack London does not in his letters readily exhibit the astonishment or dissociation or gratitude that sudden fame effects in people. He got used to the big time very quickly. He was an avid reader of Nietzsche and had come to believe in the power of Will. He believed his life was evidence of his superior strength of will. (Inevitably, the aspiring writer who communicated with him would be admonished to work hard.) Although he had managed at a late age to complete high school, he was essentially an autodidact; he had educated himself on the run, and he had the self-taught, self-made man's weakness for the Idea that Explains Everything. From the same desire to find a form for the chaos of his experience he fell in step with the slick conclusions of social Darwinism, seeing in his own travels on the road and the sea, and in the harsh snow country, confirmation of the idea of the survival of the fittest—meaning, in his Kipling-riddled mind, the best racial stock. So he was by his mid-twenties, a carrier of the fashionable and mutually exclusive ideas of his time—democratic socialism and pseudoscientific racism—in the body of his own burning vitality.

No wonder his letters are for the most part characterized by overbearing opinions. He may admit to sorrow or weariness but seldom to self-doubt. He will in 1899 confidently tell his friend Cloudsley Johns, "That the Teutonic is the dominant race of the world there is no question . . . The Negro races, the mongrel races . . . are of bad blood." In a letter of 1900 to the same friend he philosophizes, apropos his materialistic views: "The fundamental characteristic of all life is IRRITABILITY." Another quality of these letters is the love of argument, disputation. He conducts every casual correspondence with fan or critic like a debate. The need to communicate is overwhelming. He is world-famous in 1905 when he writes: "Dear Comrade, I can't read your letter. I've wasted twenty minutes, ruined my eyesight, and lost my temper and I can't make out what you have written. Try it over again and more legibly. Sincerely yours, Jack London. P.S. I can't even make out your name."

—

Jack London's strong opinions extended to the relations between the sexes. As a materialist he did not believe in romance. Already rising in his profession, he threw over the sweet and, he thought now, shallow Mabel Applegarth and went wild over a brilliant radical named Anna Strunsky, a member of a set of Bay Area bohemians, artists, writers, and intellectuals called The Crowd; but he married a bourgeois woman he did not love, Bessie Mae Maddern, because he felt they would make good biological parents and she would give him the home and the stability he needed to protect him from the voracity of his appetites and the wildness of his ways. "For a thousand reasons I think myself justified in making this marriage," he writes Anna Strunsky in April of 1900. "It will not, however, interfere much with my old life or my life as I had planned it for the future."

Inevitably, then, romance would sweep him up. In 1903, by now the father of two biologically trustworthy little girls, Joan and Becky, he fell in love with Charmian Kittredge, an editor and out-doorswoman. She too was a member of The Crowd, if less central to it than Anna Strunsky and Jack himself. Bess Maddern was jealous of the time Jack spent away from her while she was loyally keeping his home and raising their two daughters. Under the influence of the poet George Sterling, The Crowd had drifted down to Carmel and were setting up residence there, and Bess felt they had superior ways and flaunted their dislike of the plain middle class, of which she was a stubbornly satisfied member. When Jack began a clandestine affair with Charmian Kittredge ("I do not know whether I shall hear from you, whether or not you will come to me tonight," he writes in the lover's rhetoric of cosmic conviction, "but this I do know . . . it is inevitable. The hour is already too big to become anything less than the biggest. We cannot fail, diminish, fall back into night with the dawn thus in our eyes," and so on), Bess Maddern understood something had happened, though she didn't quite know with whom. She filed for separation, mistakenly naming Anna Strunsky as corespondent, although, ironically, Anna had refused to consummate her relationship with Jack because he was a married man.

All this we learn in detail from Clarice Stasz's *American Dreamers: Charmian and Jack London.* In 1905 the famous writer's divorce from a wife with two small children and his marriage to a woman, Charmian, of the advanced sort, who rode a horse astride and supported herself working in an office, made headlines and set the editorial writers to shaking their heads. Nevertheless, the marriage of Jack and Charmian London was to last until his death eleven years later, and at a level of intensity across the spectrum of emotions that marks a true match.

It is the Stasz biography's intention to show a partnership of equals that was revolutionary for its times and may still be today. I'm not sure it makes its case. There is no question that Charmian London was a remarkable woman. She was physically brave, resourceful, and in many ways ahead of her time. She was five years older than her husband but with the strong, trim, athletic body of a person much younger. She was a very good swimmer and a fine shot. She loved the outdoors and subscribed to regimens of physical fitness. She had managed as a single woman to live on the income of some small property and her own earnings at various jobs, including that of editor for the *Overland Monthly* magazine. She was a feminist proud of her mind and her independence. The 1900 model of American womanhood as pious homebody effacing herself for the sake of her family was laughable to her.

Charmian London met every challenge that her marriage to Jack London set her. He believed in physical trials, roughing it up; she used to put on boxing gloves and spar with him. She became his editor and typist, responsible for the daily twister of words that rose from his pen, including his correspondence. When the San Francisco earthquake struck, she accompanied him from Oakland when he wanted to walk the broken and burning streets. With their marriage, Jack's idea of a life of socialist crusade was somehow rationalized into the necessity to sail around the world, like Joshua Slocum. She sailed with him across the Pacific on the ill-fated, badly built ketch of his own design, the *Snark*, and turned out to be an intrepid sailor whose physical and mental ability to withstand the trials of ocean seamanship was greater than his.

Charmian lost two children at birth, one through the malpractice of the delivering doctor, and she wrote about those sorrows with honest and touching nobility. She was in fact a very good writer, and her *Log of the Snark*, as well as *The Book of Jack London*, a lesser work of her widowhood, can be read with interest today. And she was inspiring enough to him to be the model of several of his women characters—Paula, the heroine of the late novel *Little Lady of the Big House*, for example.

For all of this, however, it was not a marriage of equals. Jack wrote Charmian a most peculiar letter in July of 1903, in their first passion. In it he told her of his recurrent dream of living as one with a "great Man-Comrade," a dream he had thought would never be realized. "It was plain that . . . I could never hope to find that comradeship, that closeness, that sympathy and understanding whereby the man and I might merge and become one for love and life. How can I say what I mean? This man should be so much one with me that we could never misunderstand. . . . He should be delicate and tender, brave and game, sensitive as he pleased in the soul of him and in the body of him unfearing and unwitting of pain. Do you see, my dear one, the man I am trying to picture for you? . . . Don't you see, dear love, the all-around man I mean?"

He called her Mate-Woman and she called him Mate-Man, oddly primitive terms of their understanding of the modernity of their relationship. But she filled, as much as any person can fulfill a dream, his ideal of the womanly man that was apparently built into the structure of his psychic life. And it was this life they lived in body and spirit—his work and his political causes and his schemes and his dissolute ways, that took them on their adventures and were the primary subjects of her thought.

Charmian's life with Jack covered the period in which his socialist dreams transmuted into the consolations of rugged idealism. It was Charmian who suffered most the farce-endings of his grandiose plans. Just as he had once had to convalesce from scurvy in Alaska, now they had to sell the *Snark*, which was essentially unsailable, and take a steamer home so that he could recuperate from one or another of his increasingly frequent ailments—rotten teeth, painful hemorrhoids, fistula of the bowel, kidney stones. He took up ranching in the Sonoma Valley, buying up enormous parcels of land, breeding prize cattle, and planting crop trees, and spent another fortune building a grand manor of native stone and redwood, Wolf House, which was still incomplete after five years in the building when it mysteriously burned down. The final cruel farce was the collapse of his own vital constitution. As subject as everything else about him to the accelerated rate of his life, it decayed rapidly in his late thirties. He had vile eating habits, being given to raw duck, for example, and he was a phenomenal drinker. He smoked incessantly and took self-prescribed narcotics, against which there were then no legal restrictions, for his kidney and bowel agonies. He bloated up with edema and was insomniac, and the last pictures of him in his Baden-Powell hat and jodhpurs, gazing at the camera with a sort of Archie Bunker haplessness, mock the handsome young socialist lad, lover, and all-around hell-raiser he had been.

It was Jack London's capacity for really living in the world, for taking it on in self-conscious and often reckless acts of courage, that made him our first writer-hero. What becomes even clearer to the reader of his letters is that he was a true son of California. You can virtually map his spirit: At seventeen shipping out to Japan and the Bering Sea. At twenty-one, the portage to the Alaskan goldfields. At twenty-eight, covering the Russo-Japanese war in Korea for the Hearst papers. At thirty-two, sailing with Charmian to Tahiti and to the Marquesas, where he would trace Melville's route to the valley of the Typee. He lived for long periods in Hawaii, making friends of the landed white gentry of Honolulu and the lepers of Molokai. The flashy generation of writers after his that included Hemingway and Fitzgerald would move to Europe—to France, to Spain—from a despair of American provincialism, but Jack London was himself a provincial, of the proud California kind that finds its own path to sophistication; he lived his last decade devoting himself to his Beauty Ranch in the Sonoma Valley, and from San Francisco Bay to the Yukon to the beaches of Polynesia to the Valley of the Moon, the world he made his own was the earthquake world of the Pacific basin.

Surely his wandering and his fervent belief in the physical life couldn't have failed to influence Hemingway, whose own grim devotion to manly pursuits was even more self-conscious and was in fact a corruption of the idea, fixing, as it eventually did, on sports and ritual tests of his manhood rather than the open confrontation with nature—in snow, portage; on the high seas, a sail; in the Solomon Islands, a sojourn with the headhunters.

The other working ethic of London's life was that of the free lance. He was committed to the regimen of writing to pay the bills and was never above hacking out a good tale that he knew the market would take. Wherever he was, and however put upon, he did his thousand words a day. His letters are filled, even in the years of his greatest earnings, with boasts, vows, promises, and importunings to publishers and filmmakers from whom he wants money. The more money he made, the more surely he committed himself to enterprises that would gobble it up—the *Snark,* and then his ranch, with a labor force that was to reach fifty, the monumental Wolf House, which he was never to live in, and so on. He founded the Jack London Grape Juice Company and lost his shirt. Like Mark Twain, he backed the inventor of an unworkable typesetting machine. And like Chekhov, he carried a lot of family with him—his mother, his mother's adopted son, his estranged first wife, Bess Maddern, and their two daughters, his second wife, Charmian, and various relatives and friends, socialist comrades, and hangers-on whom he put on his payroll or who came regularly to dine at his table. Surely in this, as well as in his drinking, he had to have been a model for Scott Fitzgerald, who brought to exquisite perfection the writer's sacrifice of his talent to his expansive style of living.

But when it was all over there were fifty published books of Jack London fiction and nonfiction—five hundred articles or essays, two hundred short stories, and nineteen novels. To this day he is the most widely read American writer in the world. An earlier biographer, Andrew Sinclair—who conveys more convincingly than Ms. Stasz the complexity of London's inner torments and the finally overwhelming costs of his unresolved psychic conflicts, for instance between his socialism and his white supremacist racism, or his egalitarian ideals and his belief in himself as a Nietzschean superman, or his masculine cultishness and his feminism—points out that London was the first American to write a road novel, the first to deal with boxing as a serious subject for fiction, and the first to use the press to promote himself into mythic celebrity so as to sell his books. What is perhaps a finer epitaph are the two anthology volumes of London in the definitive Library of America series of classic American literature. They include *The Call of the Wild, White Fang,* and *The Sea Wolf,* of course; *The People of the Abyss,* his reportage on homelessness; *The Road; The Iron Heel,* his political prophecy and science fiction fantasy; *Martin Eden; John Barleycorn,* the confessions of his alcoholism; a couple of dozen stunning stories; and a handful of essays, including "Revolution," the one he used to deliver as a lecture whenever people invited him to speak.

Jack London was never an original thinker. He was a great gobbler-up of the world, physically and intellectually, the kind of writer who went to a place and wrote his dreams into it, the kind of writer who found an Idea and spun his psyche around it. He was a workaday literary genius/hack who knew instinctively that Literature was a generous host who always had room for one more at her table. He sits now below the salt, while the cooler, more sophisticated voices of Modernist irony take up the conversation.

(1988)

. . . and His Call of the Wild

T *he Call of the Wild* was Jack London's second novel, the master-piece of his early period, and an enormous commercial success. It brought him a readership that was loyal to him to the end of his life. It is still the most popular of his books, widely available in numerous editions—the one Jack London title read by nearly every American student. It is a novella in length and linearity, but a novel in feverish intention. It was published in four installments in *The Saturday Evening Post* and then in book form, by Macmillan, in the year 1903. We begin to appreciate its peculiar nature if we recall that Jack London's contemporaries were Henry James and Theodore Dreiser. This is speed-reading literature, though of an uncanny, mythic classicism. It is an action tale as topical as the big story of its time—the gold rush of 1897—though as much a tour de force of symbolic transfiguration as *Dr. Jekyll and Mr. Hyde.*

Perhaps the beginnings of his plot came to Jack London when he saw the carcasses of horses and mules covering the trail in his portage to the goldfields. The tens of thousands of gold seekers who rushed to the Klondike learned quickly that only dogs could serve for transport in the Northland. And so the market demand for sled dogs is what launches the saga of Buck, a handsome, intelligent cross between a Saint Bernard and a Scotch shepherd living in contentment on a ranch in the "sun-kissed" Santa Clara Valley of California. Buck is kidnapped by one of his owner's groundskeepers, sold to a dealer, put in a cage, and shipped by rail and sea to Dyea Beach, the stepping-off point to the Klondike. The cherished and cared for range dog of the south is clubbed into submission and left to make his bed in the snow.

The subsequent challenges, lessons, tests of courage, trials of stamina, and threats to life and limb to which Buck is exposed are the stuff of good serial writing. Like the hero of any adventure tale, he meets one challenge only to be faced with another. His life is peripatetic, he is part of a team sold from master to master, and whether they are hard but fair or simply cruel or stupid, the masters run him. Buck seems to be assailed on all sides. Both men and the dogs rise up to teach him the "law of club and fang." He learns to fight for his food, and for his place in the team; he practices cunning to avoid the dreaded club and suffers many a bloodletting and rent of fur and flesh before he becomes expert in the preferred fighting technique of the wolves and native dogs, who leap forward, fangs exposed, to cut and slash or snap, and then jump back. He learns, in this universe of primordial struggle, that the dog who loses his footing in battle loses his life, for then the whole pack moves in for the kill.

But it is not its consistent narrative advance that makes Buck's story remarkable—in 1903 every pulp writer who published knew how to keep up the action of a tale, and if he didn't his editors did. More to the point is the system of thoughts and feelings ascribed to Buck: He lives a complex spiritual life; his fate is made important to us to the same extent that our own dreams are important to us and give us conviction of our moral consequence.

It is this fact of Buck's complex spiritual life to which some of the book's first reviewers objected, on the ground that animals may have instincts but do not have thoughts. A closer look at the text, though, shows us that the psychology ascribed to Buck is generally of two kinds. The first is nothing that could not be observed, by a human, as behavior, as in this passage describing Buck's love for John Thornton, the man who saves his life:

> Buck knew no greater joy than [Thornton's] rough embrace and
> the sound of murmured oaths . . . it seemed that his heart would
> be shaken out of his body so great was its ecstasy. And . . . ,
> released, he sprang to his feet, his mouth laughing, his eyes elo-
> quent, his throat vibrant with unuttered sound, and in that fashion
> remained without movement.

In fact the book's depictions of dog behavior are both loving and
precise, though at least partially derivative. In 1907 a magazine
article in *The Independent* accused the author of plagiarizing much
of his dog lore from a nonfiction work entitled *My Dogs in the
Northland* by Edgerton R. Young. London readily admitted to rely-
ing on the information in Young's book but made a spirited denial
that this was plagiarism since the source was not a novel but a
"compilation of facts and real happenings in a non-fiction form."

The second sort of psychological life given to Buck, not humanly
observable, is species memory, or the turning of his mind under the
rigors of life to his primeval inheritance:

> Sometimes as [Buck] crouched there, blinking dreamily at the
> flames, it seemed that the flames were of another fire, and that
> . . . he saw another and different man . . . before him. This
> other man . . . was all but naked, a ragged and fire-scorched skin
> hanging part way down his back, but on his body there was much
> hair . . . matted into almost a thick fur. He did not stand erect.

Man and dog are here together put back into prehistory, one of the
moments of metaphorical abutment in which the book abounds.
The law of the club and the law of the fang are one and the same,
which is to say that in this primeval life of nature man and dog are
morally indistinguishable—the call of the wild calls us all. We are
dealing in this instance with not a literal dog but a mythopoetic
thesis.

As far back as Aesop, of course, authors have used animals as
stand-ins for people. Animal heroes and villains confer a moral

clarity; they are the gamier taste of human innocence and evil, gullibility and cunning, cravenness and nobility. They are necessarily given to edification. One would need a scholar to go through the literature and annotate the exceptional animals, the ones who are not flat characters, in E. M. Forster's definition—meaning those not exhausted by one humor, one governing self-expression in any and all circumstances—but who, like Buck, are given more complicated work to do. The fact is that today the tradition of the adult animal tale in America has virtually disappeared; it is a less possible literary expedient in the aftermath of two world wars, their attendant modernist ironies, and the rise of Walt Disney. But when Jack London wrote, in the days of Baden-Powell, formulator of the Boy Scout ethos, Americans from Teddy Roosevelt on down took their animals seriously, as Native Americans still do, and it was possible for animals to speak for us and live for us instructively as fables of ourselves—with thoughts or without them.

The book is driven not, cheaply, by potboiling hazards to the life of its hero but by its author's voice. The voice of the book is the voice of insistent wisdom. It speaks to intone what is momentous. It will depict a real, dog-behaving dog and then enlarge or blur his lineaments to mythic dimensions. Events are arranged into a deepening implication. The call of the wild is given as leitmotiv; it returns more and more insistently with clearer and clearer resolution as Buck acclimates to brute existence—until finally he encounters in a pristine northern forest the call incarnate, a wolf who will offer him the primordial life he has envisioned in his man/wolf dreams. The real suspense of the tale is not *Will the dog survive?* but *What is his philosophical destiny?* When he finds the love of John Thornton, a man as noble as he is, Buck struggles against the call of the wild; he is conflicted. But when Thornton is killed by Yeehat Indians in an act of basic savagery no different from that of a wolf pack, Buck takes his revenge, mourns and howls in the night, and moves out of our sight once and for all to run, mythologically, with the pack.

The dream life of our atavistic selves as Jack London writes it is a discipline of thought and feeling quite proscribed—as the book's universe is proscribed in reiterated images of cold and darkness and snow and ice and meat and blood. The deceptively simple adventure tale is a mythic rendering, as in Ovid, where for reward or punishment beings are transformed, people become animals or trees or snakes or birds or bats. In this instance, on a dream field of wilderness a self-realization is achieved, which is to say the injustice done the hero is absorbed and metabolized by him and he finds his transfiguration. Buck is carefully made to be noble. He is physically impressive, like all literary nobility, but also a gallant, loyal creature, well disposed to man and dog until he's forced for his life to be otherwise. He learns, he grows, he develops. He is in fact rounder than most of the human characters of the book, who are quite flat in their villainy or stupidity. This is the sort of joke that builds a literary work into its realization. *The Call of the Wild* may well constitute a parody of the bildungsroman, the novel concerned with the sentimental education of its hero, not only because the hero in question is a dog but also because his education decivilizes him to the savage wolfhood of his ancestors.

I don't mean to say that the work is satirical or that it in any way questions itself as solemnly intended. On the contrary, this is Jack London's fervently American variant of the novel of sentimental education. It is perhaps his fatherless life of bitter self-reliance in late-nineteenth-century America that he transmutes here—though this is not the way it does us any good to read it. It seems more relevantly his mordant parable of the thinness of civilization, the brutality ready to spring up through our institutions, the failure of the human race to evolve truly from its primeval beginnings. It derives from Jack London's Marxism the idea of the material control of our natures, and from his Darwinism the conviction that life triumphant belongs to the most fit. This is not a sweet idea for a book, it is rather the kind of concept to justify tyrannies and the need of repressive social institutions to keep people from tearing themselves to bits. But London's Nietzschean superdog has our admiration, if the truth be told. For as grim as its implications are, the tale never forgets its sources as a magazine frontier romance. It leaves us with satisfaction at its outcome, a story well and truly told. It is Jack London's hack genius that makes us cheer for his Buck and want to lope with him in happy, savage honor back to the wild, running and howling with the pack.

(1990)

THEODORE DREISER
BOOK ONE AND
BOOK TWO

Theodore Dreiser: Book One

Theodore Dreiser was born in Terre Haute, Indiana, in 1871. His father was a German Catholic immigrant, embittered by hard luck in business. His mother, by contrast, had seemingly endless resources of courage and hope for her ten children despite the staggering burden of bearing and raising them in poverty. The family moved from one Indiana town to another as the father lost or found employment. In Volume 1 of Dreiser's autobiography, *Dawn*, he remembers scavenging along the railroad tracks for coal for the family stove; but he testifies also to the joyful sensuality of his child's feelings for life and the natural world around him.

At the age of fifteen, influenced by the accounts of some of his older brothers and sisters, Theodore went off alone to Chicago—the same sort of journey, and made for the same reason, as that undertaken by the heroine of *Sister Carrie*. He found work as a dishwasher and busboy and then as a shipping clerk. After an interval at Indiana University in Bloomington, financed by a former schoolteacher who believed in his potential, he returned to his romance with the city of Chicago as a bill collector, real estate clerk, and laundry-truck driver.

But he had vague ambitions of writing. He had delivered newspapers as a child and had come to associate with the life of a reporter all the drama and glory of the catastrophes of history and the doings of great men. His first newspaper job was at the Chicago *Herald*—dispensing toys for the needy at Christmas. But eventually he was hired as a cub reporter for the Chicago *Globe* and subsequently went on to St. Louis to become a feature writer for the *Globe-Democrat*. After reviewing in absentia a theatrical performance that turned out not to have occurred, he felt it wise to leave St. Louis. He found a job with the *Dispatch* in Pittsburgh, where, since it was the aftermath of the Homestead strike, in which armies of Pinkerton detectives and striking steelworkers had fought pitched battles, he began to appreciate some of the problems inherent in American economic life.

In the second volume of his autobiography, *Newspaper Days*, Dreiser acknowledges the formative influence of his fellow reporters and editors—cynics, boulevardiers, and drunks though many of them were. "They did not believe, as I still did, that there was a fixed moral order in the world which one contravened at his peril." But while he absorbed their ideas and attitudes he seems to have been immune to their world-weary resources. Here is his description of the character of his young self: "Chronically nebulous, doubting, uncertain, I stared and stared at everything, only wondering, not solving." This happens also to be a perfect description of the state of readiness in a novelist.

Yet it was not until he was working in New York as a magazine editor—by now married to Sara White, a schoolteacher he had met at the Chicago World's Fair—that Dreiser even thought of writing fiction. A friend of his, Arthur Henry, an Ohio journalist, had encouraged him to write stories and then challenged him to write a novel. Henry, to his credit, had recognized in Dreiser's work as a feature writer the capacity of the novelist. And so in 1899, Theodore Dreiser, age twenty-eight, wrote the title, "Sister Carrie" on a piece of paper, and having no idea what it meant, proceeded to compose the book to find out.

It is not difficult to find in *Sister Carrie* the circumstantial details that Dreiser brought to it from his own life: what it means to be in wonder and awe of a great city in which you're looking for work, or to be desperately hungry and down on your luck and homeless, or to be on the way up the business ladder, a young man dressed in the latest fashion and knowing how to endear himself to young women. One of Dreiser's sisters had run off to Toronto with a married man, just as Carrie does to Montreal, and the married man had turned out to have stolen money from his employer, just as Carrie's lover George Hurstwood is made to do. The Chicago of the novel is the Chicago Dreiser knew in his youth and is painstakingly accurate in its references to streets, hotels, and restaurants. The New York where Carrie and Hurstwood play out their love affair is one you may trust down to the last streetlamp.

But none of this accounts for the composition—what the act of writing creates. We may hope to sense what this is by reflecting on F. O. Matthiessen's statement, in his authoritative critical biography *Theodore Dreiser*, that Dreiser was "virtually the first major American writer whose family name was not English or Scotch-Irish." An outsider because of his German background, his poverty, his limited parochial school education, Dreiser sprang to being as an artist independent of the prevailing literary and cultural values and tastes that might otherwise have formed him. He wrote about what he had seen as a working reporter—and he had seen a lot. He stood outside the governing New England influence that George Santayana called "the genteel tradition"—a tradition whose end result, according to Matthiessen, "is to make art an adornment rather than an organic expression of life, to confuse it with politeness and delicacy . . . and to think of literature as somehow dependent upon the better born groups of richer standing."

Eighty years later our literary history has absorbed the work of James T. Farrell, Richard Wright, Nelson Algren, Saul Bellow—to mention just those ethnic and lower-depth writers out of Chicago—and the immigrant impudence is itself part of the prevailing culture. But in 1900 the first publisher to see the manuscript of *Sister Carrie*, Harper Brothers, turned it down on the grounds that it was not "sufficiently delicate to depict without offense to the reader the continued illicit relations of the heroine." And the publisher who accepted it, Doubleday, Page, published it with trepidation, and therefore badly. It came out in 1900, sold less than seven hundred copies, and created for Dreiser the reputation of naturalist-barbarian that followed him down the years.

What was the nature of the book's offense? In what way did it lack sufficient delicacy? Sara White Dreiser felt the trouble lay partly in the references to the sexual lives of the characters. Dreiser struck all of these he could find before submitting the book to Doubleday. Literary scholars tell us that both Mrs. Dreiser and Arthur Henry were intimately involved in the editing of the manuscript after the Harper rejection. The commendable scholarship of the Dreiserians of the University of Pennsylvania Press, which in 1981 published a version of the uncut manuscript, makes it possible to see, however, that even the uncut *Sister Carrie* was never sexually explicit nor less than circumspect in its depictions of physical life.

But Dreiser's wife and friend were closer to the mark when they urged him not to leave the reader at the end of the book with the impression that Carrie was to be rewarded for her life of illicit relation. Dreiser wrote according to the aesthetic principle of Realism, which proposes that the business of fiction is not to draw an idealized picture of human beings for the instruction or sentimental satisfaction of readers, but rather to portray life as it is really lived under specific circumstances of time and place, and to show how people actually think and feel and why they do what they do. But the young author had also chosen, consciously or unconsciously, to build his realistic novel on one of the oldest narrative conventions in literature—a convention, moreover, right off the shelf of literary gentility. Dreiser made the changes asked of him; but the structural parody of *Sister Carrie* is its pointed offense—one which no amount of judicious editing could soften.

Consider that in Chapter 1, before her train even reaches Chicago, the eighteen-year-old Carrie, a "half-equipped little knight . . . venturing to reconnoitre the mysterious city and dreaming wild dreams," is picked up by a traveling salesman who sits in the coach seat behind hers and, assuming theology's favored position for the Devil, leans forward and whispers into her ear. The assault upon innocence is a staple of Christian melodrama; as a narrative convention it looks back at least as far as the first novel in English, Samuel Richardson's *Pamela*, whose heroine is exercised in defense of her virtue for well over three hundred pages. Our Carrie doesn't make it past page 64. Unable to find a decent job, overwhelmed by the rude rush and merciless dazzle of an urban society, she moves in with the importunate salesman, Charlie Drouet, and improves her fortunes materially by her act. Furthermore, Drouet is shown to be not a bad fellow, only somewhat shallow and insensitive.

Living unwed with Drouet and then, in a somewhat more complicated situation, with the hero of the book, George Hurstwood, Carrie hardly suffers any of the standard fates the convention requires. Dreiser saw to it that she would not end up happy, but neither is she punished or repentant. What is more important, the author never suggests that her alternatives, had she been capable of choosing them, would have given her a finer life or made her a better person.

Of course Dreiser is not in spirit a parodist. He's the least ironical of our major writers and there is reason to doubt from the evidence of *Sister Carrie* that he has even the hope of wit. What he has rather is a concern for the moral consequence of life that is so pervasive as to constitute a vision. But it is unmediated by piety. All God can do in *Sister Carrie* is provide a soup line for someone who's down and out. He is not presumed by any of the characters to provide guidance, let alone redemption. He is not indicated by even one fully functioning conscience. And those characters who are wronged—Hurstwood's wife and children, for example—are themselves motivated by material values; they are as single-mindedly ambitious, and governed by the same sensitivity to wealth and status, as everyone else.

And here we may begin to hope to locate the achievement of this novel. There is a remarkable moment of transition when it becomes

clear that Carrie will lose her virginity. We are immediately taken
into the mind of her older sister Minnie, a drab, spiritless woman,
married to an immigrant who cleans refrigerator cars at the stock-
yards for a living. Minnie has not been particularly generous or
supportive to her younger sister—families and, by implication, the
values of family life do not come out well in *Sister Carrie*—but she
is concerned enough about Carrie's fate to have a troubled dream
as she falls asleep. In her dream she sees Carrie disappear forever
into the dark pit of some sort of water-ridden coal mine. Characteristically, Dreiser chooses the right direction for Hell, but his metaphor has a superseding value. The black coal mine is perdition in
its industrial form. And it is solely in the modern industrial world,
without reference to any other state of existence than the material,
that Dreiser finds the government of our moral being.

The Dreiserian universe is composed of merchants, workers, club
men, managers, actors, salesmen, doormen, cops, derelicts—a
Balzacian population unified by the rules of commerce and the ideals of property and social position. "The true meaning of money yet
remains to be popularly explained and comprehended," Dreiser
says at the beginning of Chapter 7, and proceeds, with *Sister Carrie*,
to give us the best explanation we have had. It is not merely that his
characters must display it if they have it, work for it, steal, or beg
for it if they haven't: their very beings are contingent upon it—who
they are in the character of their souls.

When we first meet George Hurstwood he is a virile man of the
world, with a cosmopolitan charm and an intelligence competent to
all the demands that his life might place on him—exactly the char-
acteristics that attract Carrie. But after he wins her—having to go to
great lengths to get her away from Drouet—and is living with her
in New York, his powers fade and he enters into a slow, terrible
decline of spirit. In the material world, the stature of a man is in his
exterior supports. His passion for Carrie has removed Hurstwood
from his job, from the respect of his peers, and from the accoutre-
ments of position—house, family, bank account. Without these he is

without will. He is simply not the same man. His love for Carrie cannot sustain him—indeed, it collapses along with his income.

Carrie, for her part, is emphasized to be a passive individual who comes into animation under the attentions of others. She never thinks about anything she hasn't seen. She is a heroine who goes through her story without an idea in her head. If Dreiser is telling here of a sentimental education, Carrie's teachers are not primarily the men who keep her but other women—the succession of neighbors and friends who instruct her in the longing for clothes, jewels, apartments, and in all the emblems of taste and fashion. It is these things that arouse her passion and delineate her possibilities. And when, under the pressure of circumstance, she discovers her talent for acting, it will be seen that her success springs not from any force of creativity, innate and substantive, but from the fact that her face and demeanor so well represent "the world's longing." It is Carrie as representation of all desire, a poignant reflection of the entire society, that makes her a star and causes people to pay money to see her. Dreiser gives this crucial observation to the one person in the book who is capable of standing in judgment of the culture he lives in, the remote Mr. Ames, a character said to have been modeled on Thomas Alva Edison. "The world is always struggling to express itself," Ames tells Carrie. "Your face . . . [is] a thing the world likes to see because it's a natural expression of its longing."

Longing, the hope for fulfillment, is the one unwavering passion of the world's commerce. Dreiser is of two minds about this passion. To a populace firmly in the grip of material existence, the desire for something more is a destructive energy that can never be exhausted; it is doom. Hurstwood, whose success as manager of a high-class drinking establishment is not sufficient, fixes his further ambition on Carrie, and is ruined. But the desire for something more, the longing for fulfillment, is also hope, and therefore innocence, a sort of redemption. Carrie, at the top of her profession, is left looking for something more, and though we understand she will never find it—no more than Hurstwood has—her recognition that she is unfulfilled is the closest thing to grace in the Dreiser theology.

H. L. Mencken, although a great friend and champion of Dreiser's, felt the author had made a serious compositional error by giving so much space, in a novel about Carrie, to the fate of Hurstwood. Mencken believed this ruined the organic unity of the book. It is true there are no more graphic and stunning scenes than those that follow Hurstwood down to dereliction. But the case is overstated. Dreiser's panoptic vision encompasses more than the story of one or another individual. George Hurstwood's fall propels Carrie Meeber's rise. As Einstein taught, the energy of the universe is never exhausted, only transformed and recycled. Carrie discovers her ability to earn money because Hurstwood has lost his. Together they describe all the possibilities of material fate, lonely death, enormous success, and in a world in which everyone is alone with his own ambition, the moral consequence is the same.

It is astonishing to consider how—in this big realistic novel, which takes us into three cities and effectively portrays most of the classes of American society, a novel in which we are witness to physical degradation, homelessness, unremitting labor, and violent strikes at the one extreme, and fine living, glamorous well-being, and wealth at the other, and through which a seemingly endless cast of characters appear fully animated in their surroundings of streets, tenements, saloons, office buildings, trains, hotels, theaters —it is astounding how hermetic this novel is. What a closed and suffocating America Dreiser seals us in! The self-educated immigrant's son, a naïf who stared and wondered at everything, managed to connect it all in as unitary a vision as has been produced by American literature. He is said to be a clumsy, cumbersome writer, but the clarity and consistency of his vision is a function of his craft. It comes of a control of recurrent imagery and reiterated observation. It comes of a narrative voice that is older, wiser, and more compassionate than we have any right to expect from a first novelist in his twenties. It is a result of the rate of stately progress of the events of the story, and of the attention given to every phase of growth in the feelings of the major characters—which brilliantly exceeds, in its patience, the magnitude of their minds or the originality of their problems. There is nothing clumsy about any of this, nor anything but genius in the vision that comes off the pages of *Sister Carrie* and into each and every one of us.

(1983)

. . . and Book Two

As an artist, Theodore Dreiser (1871–1945) struggled with two distinct centuries. His younger contemporary F. Scott Fitzgerald claimed there were no second acts in American lives, but *Sister Carrie* was written in 1899 and *An American Tragedy,* Dreiser's other masterpiece, in 1926. These towers rise from a structure of sturdy novels, volumes of autobiography, studies of representative men and women, polemical works, plays, poems, stories, and innumerable newspaper and magazine pieces, an early example of which is an account of the working life of New York harbor pilots as they go out under sail to meet the transatlantic steamers. Yet Dreiser was still alive to read of the dropping of the bomb on Hiroshima.

His full and tempestuous life seems almost to have run backward. One of the astonishing things about *Sister Carrie,* written by a twenty-eight-year-old, is the voice of the book, which is that of a septuagenarian. Where did this first novelist find the wisdom and voice of an elder to detect the insatiable longing that characterizes the American soul?

Apparently Dreiser's advantage, as one of ten children of an impoverished German immigrant, was in being born old. As he matured, he became younger and more disorderly. He had married early but soon separated from his wife. Because his novel had sold under five hundred copies, he was aware of his painful obscurity as the younger brother of Paul Dresser, a popular songwriter celebrated to this day in Terre Haute as the composer of the Indiana state song. Dreiser suffered deeply from the provincialism that found *Sister Carrie* the unforgivable work of a barbarian naturalist; but he took a job as editor of *Butterick's*, a slick magazine, where he energetically enforced just those editorial strictures of mindless gentility he had outraged as a writer. He was to lose this job because of his too assiduous pursuit of the seventeen-year-old daughter of a colleague—an affection that foretold his middle age, when he was a rampant satyr deviously conducting several affairs simultaneously. His appetite for food, for drink, for fame, grew equally voracious.

Dreiser was a Spencerian mechanist but found in the godless universe of the surviving fittest the reason for transports of mystical conviction. The sight of a pretty sunset made him weep. In the 1930s he went to Russia and detested what he found there—which, according to the retrogressive direction of his life, meant, inevitably, he would join the Communist party. The more he wrote, and the wealthier his writings made him, the more insecure both he and his reputation became. He was as self-obsessed as any writer but could never work through his own disorder to compose himself properly in the public eye. A large, horse-faced man with a misaligned gaze, he lacked glamour. He could not make a creation of himself, as Hemingway did, as Fitzgerald did—his younger competitors who surpassed him also in irony and the modish literature of the unsaid. Dreiser's heavyweight novels were the literature of the everything said.

By the last decade of his life he was making public pronouncements on subjects of which he had little or no understanding. He was winging off telegrams to the president of the United States on matters of national policy. He had expended himself on radical causes, which America will suffer in its students but not in its writers. He stooped now to expressing his bigotries—his dislike of Jews, though it was by then widely known what anti-Semitism was doing to Jews in Europe, or his hatred of the British upper classes, for whose retribution he hoped Hitler would invade England.

Toward the end, not only was he talking about all the big questions of the nineteenth century—Science versus Religion, Whither the Universe?—but talking as if he were the first and only one who had ever thought of these things, a sophomore at seventy. And in his final days he felt misunderstood, unloved, and abandoned, like a child who lives in a comfortable home and is doted on by its parents. Adored by his longtime companion and second wife, Helen Richardson, he said to yet another lady a few days before he died, "I am the loneliest man in the world."

So it is the young Dreiser who necessarily interests us most, the fully formed author, the pre-matured genius. His early life had taught him that in America wealth displays itself obsessionally in the eyes of the poor, the golden glitter of the inside transfixes the outsider. In no subsequent work was he to use this ingenuous vision to greater effect, or to see more deeply into the Republic, than in *Sister Carrie.*

What did this book cost him? What were the consequences to his life? Now we have the most authoritative answer, Dreiser's own. A manuscript long alluded to by his biographers, it was published by the University of Pennsylvania Press under the title *An Amateur Laborer* some eighty years after it was written. Incomplete, but bolstered by fragments of chapters and unincorporated passages, it is Dreiser's frank account of his life in Brooklyn and New York in the year 1903, the aftermath of *Carrie's* disastrous publication, when he had lost his ability to write and to earn a living, and thought seriously of suicide.

"Mine was a serious case of neurasthenia—or nervous prostration," he tells us, writing in 1904, the year of his recovery. "It had begun with the conclusion of a novel which I had written three years before and which exhausted me greatly. . . . I was morbid, had fearful dreams, slept very little. . . . I was constantly most gloomy and depressed—almost to a state of tears. . . . My nerves began to hurt me, particularly in the ends of my fingers in which I felt genuine pain. . . . I began to have the idea, or the almost irre-sistible impulse to turn around in a ring. That is, if I were sitting in a chair, I would want to keep turning to the right—an involuntary nervous discharge of will . . . almost making it impossible for me not to do so. Then too my eyes began to hurt me and I felt as if the columns of the paper or book I was reading were crooked."

But, characteristically, Dreiser is less interested in the psychologi-cal than in the material terms of the problem—how life appears to and is understood by one who has dropped out of it. Picture him, age thirty-one, well over six feet tall and weighing under one hun-dred forty pounds. He has given up on his second novel, "Jennie Gerhardt," after three years of stymied effort and of fitful drifting up and down the Eastern Seaboard. He and his wife have sepa-rated. He has taken a room in a shabby boardinghouse in a slum of Brooklyn. With just a few dollars left to his name, he begins to resort to the strategies of poverty, subsisting on bread and milk, tramping the pavement to save carfare as he looks for work, even scavenging food from the garbage of the street. He suffers bitterly when a gust of raw February wind blows his hat away and he can't retrieve it from the subway construction site in which it has disap-peared. This is Dreiser, the once-successful young newspaperman and the author of a novel mighty enough to have secured his repu-tation among such literary lights as Frank Norris.

There is something eerily familiar in this torment. Having de-cided his only chance for survival is to get work as a laborer of some sort, to work with his hands since he can no longer use his brain, Dreiser applies for a position with the Metropolitan Street Railway system as a motorman or conductor. Didn't Hurstwood, the doomed descending hero of his novel, work at just such a job? Dreiser is turned down by the street railway people, thus suffering as well the experience of Carrie, who early in the novel is humili-ated when she applies for an unskilled job and is turned down for lack of qualification. Time and time again throughout *An Amateur Laborer* Dreiser seems to discover with a shock what he has already invented or known in *Sister Carrie*. "What kind of a world is it," he wonders, "wherein one is always struggling to keep his head above water." And watching a procession of motorists out for a drive and feeling toward them a scornful sense of superiority, he says, "Rail as I would, the differences of life were largely based on materials, and [those] who had them could afford to let the beggars down."

F. O. Matthiessen points out in his critical biography of Dreiser that the picture of society invoked by this author is one "in which there are no real equals, and no equilibrium but only people moving *up* and *down*." That he is enacting with his life just these cycles of his fiction, Dreiser seems to be quite unaware in this autobiography. Here is, possibly, one of the great literary revelations of writer's block, that unable to find justice, or mercy, for his book, the writer will turn language into his own flesh and perform its events. Every major work of art is a transgression, but the artist is not necessarily, by nature, a transgressor. All his life Dreiser produced books from the war with himself, and even after the successful surmounting of his trials in *An Amateur Laborer*, his self-punishment continued: Up he rose to the precise position of success, a slick-magazine editor at *Butterick's*, that reproached and denied his belief in himself as a writer.

Yet the struggle he describes in this account is valiant and even cunning. Turned down again and again for every job he can think of, too proud to accept charity or get help from any of his brothers or sisters, he goes to see the general passenger agent of the New York Central and, presenting himself as a gentleman, he asks for a laborer's job on the railroad for its therapeutic value. As someone recovering his health, he thinks some form of outdoor work will do him good. He has intuited that the way to find employment is to seem not to need it.

The ruse is successful, but before he can take up his new job (at fifteen cents an hour) he happens to run into his older brother Paul in front of the Imperial Hotel on Broadway. The famous songwriter sizes things up rather quickly, takes charge of his cadaverous but proud sibling, feeds him a good dinner, gives him money, buys him a new suit of clothes, and books him for an all-paid residency at Muldoon's Sanitarium in Westchester, just north of White Plains, a health resort for wealthy men. We begin at this point in the narrative to perceive the key coordinates of Dreiser's up-and-down universe. Previously, he has stayed a few nights at the Mills Hotel on Bleecker Street (the structure still stands, under a different name), where some fifteen hundred men down on their luck idle their time away in musty cell-like rooms whose walls do not touch the ceiling or floor as a preventive measure against suicide. This is the depth of social dereliction (rent: twenty cents a day) from which Dreiser is suddenly, and fantastically, passed to Muldoon's spa, a rustic retreat of the idle rich.

The young author undergoes Muldoon's treatment, a vigorous regimen of early-morning showers, throwing and catching medicine balls, hiking, riding, accompanied by a relentless program of verbal abuse at the hands of Mr. Muldoon himself, a former champion wrestler who has perceived that the public browbeating of successful men who pay for the privilege is actually good for their characters—an early form of est, perhaps, and one which Dreiser both resents and comes to appreciate. As for his fellow residents in this odd place, he seems to find them, at least by implication, no more estimable or interesting or brilliant than the miserable wretches lying about the precincts of the Mills Hotel.

The large middle world, neither destitute nor privileged, is of course that of the ordinary working man, and once Dreiser leaves the spa, a few pounds heavier and somewhat less insomniac, he belatedly takes up his day job working in the carpentry shop of the Central, along the Hudson at Spuyten Duyvil. He works hard hauling lumber and cleaning the wood shavings off the floor and comes to study the various men he works with—the manly foreman Mike Burke, John the engineer, Henry the watchman—but if he hopes for a romantic affirmation of the honest working man, he does not find it so that he can believe it. The railroad men are generally unimaginative, unaspiring, terribly reduced in liveliness by the deadly and repetitive rituals of their work; they seem content with too little, and they lack wonder for "the mystery of life."

It is perhaps inevitable that as he identifies, finally, with none of the representative societies in which he has found himself, Dreiser should recover his own functioning identity as an artist. In all his surroundings, he has kept his critical distance, and this, at least, even in the depths of his mental terrors and impoverishment, has remained his undulled writer's faculty. Belonging not to Mills, not to Muldoon's, and not to the world between, he has used himself scientifically, as explorer in the ideas and experiences they have to offer. By 1904, when he is writing this account, he is physically and mentally restored and capable of turning out some really beautiful descriptions of New York at the turn of the century—the Hudson River at Spuyten Duyvil, the village of Kingsbridge, the view of Manhattan from Fort Lee, the hills of Westchester looking the broad way down to Long Island Sound.

But he does not finish the book—we have only the first twenty-four chapters—and the good editors of the volume, Richard W. Dowell, James L. W. West, and Neda M. Westlake, do not hazard a guess as to why. But I will. Along about Chapter 20, the transitions begin to thicken, blur the story, and turn it into that bane of biographers, unsignified experiences whose only narrative justification is that they happened. We are at the point when the outcome of the tale is assured. Dreiser has touched upon all the shock points of his sensibility, and now ordinary working men, a landlady, and, most especially, a good-looking landlady's daughter have moved in and taken possession of the mind that in the depths of illness was filled only with itself. There was no tragedy waiting at the end of this book, no loss, only, possibly, discretion.

But Dreiser was to mine the materials of *An Amateur Laborer* for many of his subsequent works—as the editors take pains to document in their wonderful enterprise. Here, recovered, is Dreiser's first fall from the heights of *Sister Carrie,* and his standing up and his dusting himself off. Young Dreiser, whose life of hazard is just beginning.

(1983)

ERNEST HEMINGWAY
R.I. P.

E arly in his career Ernest Hemingway devised the writing strategies he would follow for life: when composing a story he
would withhold mention of its central problem; when writing a
novel he would implant it in geography and, insofar as possible, he
would know what time it was on every page; when writing anything he would construct the sentences so as to produce an emotion
not by claiming it but by rendering precisely the experience to
cause it. What he made of all this was a rigorous art of compressive
power, if more suited to certain emotions than to others. He was
unquestionably a genius, but of the kind that advertises its limits.
Critics were on to these from the very beginning, but in the for-
ward-looking 1920s, they joined his readers to make him the writer
for their time. His stuff was new. It moved. There was on every
page of clear prose an implicit judgment of all other writing. The
Hemingway voice hated pretense and cant and the rhetoric they
rode in on.

The source of his material and spring to his imagination was his
own life. Issues of intellect—history, myth, society—were beside
the point. It was what his own eyes saw and heart felt that he cured
into fiction. Accordingly he lived his life to see and feel as much as
possible. There was no place on earth he was not at home, except
perhaps his birthplace. His parents' middle western provincialism

made independence an easy passage for him. He married young and fathered a child—the traditional circumstances for settling down—and took his family with him to Europe in pursuit of excitements. He skied in the Austrian Alps, entrained to Paris for the bicycle races or prizefights, crossed the Pyrenees for the bullfights, and made urgent side trips to mountain villages for the fishing or shooting. In America, too, he drove back and forth from Idaho or Wyoming to Florida, never renting a place to live in for more than a season. He was divorced and remarried, with more children, before he bought a place of his own in Key West. But there was better fishing in Cuba, and a woman he secretly wooed there who was to become his third wife—and so on. It was Flaubert who said a writer has to sit quietly in one place, rooted in boredom, to get his work done. Hemingway lived in a kind of nomadic frenzy, but the work poured out of him. The stories and pieces and novels were done in longhand in the mornings, at whatever makeshift table he could find in a room away from his family.

—

As his fame grew he was able, in this or that remote paradise he had found, to demolish his solitude by summoning friends or colleagues from other parts of the world. And they came, at whatever inconvenience to themselves, to fish or hunt or ride with him, but most important to drink with him. He had sporting friends, military friends, celebrity friends, literary friends, and friends from the local saloon. He was forever making friendships and breaking them, imagining affronts, squaring off in his heavyweight crouch. Most people are quiet in the world, and live in it tentatively, as if it is not theirs. Hemingway was its voracious consumer. People of every class were drawn to this behavior, and to the boasting, charming, or truculent boyishness of his ways, and to his ritual celebration of his appetites.

By and large he worked from life on a very short lead time. He wrote *The Sun Also Rises* while still seeing many of the people in Paris on whom he modeled its characters, and though it took him ten years to use his World War I experiences for *A Farewell to Arms,* by the time of the civil war in Spain he was making trips there knowing he was collecting the people, incidents, and locales for *For Whom the Bell Tolls,* a novel he completed in 1939, within months of the war's end. Only illness cut down his efficiency, or more often physical accidents, of which he had a great many; he ran cars into ditches and broke bones, or cut himself with knives, or scratched his eyes. But with World War II his ability to work quickly from life declined, and with it the justification of his techniques. Though he was prominently a correspondent in that war, the only novel he produced from it was the very weak *Across the River and into the Trees,* and that was not published until 1950. People noted his decline and attributed it to the corruption of fame, but in the last decade of his life he wrote *A Moveable Feast,* a memoir of his early days in Paris (published posthumously in 1964), and *The Old Man and the Sea,* and seemed to have found again what he could do.

Hemingway talked of suicide all his life before he committed it. In 1954 his proneness to accident culminated in not one but two airplane crashes in East Africa, where he had gone to hunt, and which left him with the concussion, crushed vertebrae, burns, and internal injuries that turned him, in his fifties, into an old man. From a distance the physical punishment his body received during his lifetime seems to have been half of something, a boxing match with an invisible opponent, perhaps. His mind was never far from killing, neither in actuality, as he hunted or ran off to wars, nor in his work. He went after animals all his life. He shot lion and leopard and kudu in Africa, and grizzly bear in the Rockies, he shot grouse in Wyoming and pigeon in France; wherever he was, he took what was available. And after he killed something, it was not necessarily past his attention. His biographer Carlos Baker tells of the day, in Cuba, when Hemingway hooked and fought and landed a 512-pound marlin. He brought it to port in triumph, receiving the noisy congratulations of friends and acquaintances. But this was not, apparently, enough. After a night of drunken celebration, at two or three that morning, he was seen back at the dock, all alone under the moon, the great game fish hanging upside down on block and tackle; he was using it for a punching bag.

Since Hemingway's death in 1961, his estate and his publishers, Charles Scribner's Sons, have been catching up to him, issuing the work which, for one reason or another, he did not publish in his lifetime. He held back *A Moveable Feast* out of concern for the feelings of the people in it who might still be alive. But about the novel *Islands in the Stream* he seems to have had editorial misgivings. Even more deeply in this category is *The Garden of Eden,* which he began in 1946 and worked on intermittently in the last fifteen years of his life and left unfinished. It is a highly readable story, if not possibly the book he envisioned. As published, it is composed of thirty short chapters running to about seventy thousand words. A publisher's note advises that "some cuts" have been made in the manuscript, but according to Mr. Baker's biography, at one point a revised manuscript of the work ran to forty-eight chapters and two hundred thousand words, so the publisher's note is disingenuous. In an interview with *The New York Times,* a Scribner's editor admitted to taking out a subplot in rough draft that he felt had not been integrated into the "main body" of the text, but this cut reduced the book's length by two-thirds.

———

The hero of this radically weeded *Garden of Eden* is David Bourne, a young novelist and veteran of World War I, who is traveling with his wife, Catherine, through Spain and France in the 1920s. The couple are on their honeymoon. In their small black Bugatti, they drive from the seaport village of Le Grau-du-Roi, where their stay has been idyllic, to Madrid, where the first shadows appear on their relationship. Catherine evinces jealousy of his writing. At the same time she demands experimentation in their lovemaking—she wants them to pretend that she is the boy and he is the girl. At Aigues-Mortes, in France, she has her hair cut short, and later she insists that he have his cut by the same hairdresser in a match to hers, so that he will look like her. David complies in this too, though not without some resistance and a foreboding of the ultimate corruption of the marriage.

Going on to La Napoule, near Cannes, they engage rooms in a very small hotel, where it is quiet because it is summer, the off-season in the south of France. One of the rooms is for David to write in. He has just published his war novel in America and received in the forwarded mail the press clippings and publisher's letter telling him he is a success. This news disturbs Catherine. The differences between them sharpen as she presumes to tell him the only subject worth writing about is their life together on their honeymoon.

One day, drinking at the café terrace of their hotel, they attract the attention of a beautiful young woman named Marita, who is very impressed by this darkly tanned couple with their newly bleached, almost white hair and French fisherman shirts, linen trousers, and espadrilles. She moves to their hotel. Catherine fulfills David's forebodings by commencing an affair with Marita. In further sign of her instability, she encourages David to embark on his own erotic relationship with the woman, who makes it easy by privately confessing to him that she has fallen in love with both of them. He succumbs. The ménage swims from the deserted beach coves of the area and sunbathes nude. David sleeps with one or the other as they designate in their time-sharing with him. Every day consists of a good deal of drinking—of martinis, which David himself mixes and garnishes with garlic olives at the small hotel bar, or absinthe, or Haig pinchbottle and Perrier, or Tavel, or carefully prepared Tom Collinses. The mixing and consuming of drinks is the means they seem to have chosen to adjust to the impact of their acts and conversation on one another.

It is Catherine who begins to come apart spectacularly under the strain. Becoming, in turn, bitter or remorseful, she either excoriates David for his relationship with Marita or condemns herself for making a mess of everything. As a defense against the situation, and what he perceives as his wife's clearly accelerating mental illness, he begins to write the story he has been resisting for years, the "hard" story, he calls it, based on his life as a boy in East Africa with his white-hunter father. This story gradually intrudes on the main narrative as the boy David sights the bull elephant with enormous tusks that his father and an African assistant are looking for; he reports his sighting and lives to regret it, as the father tracks down the great beast and destroys it. The climax of the novel has to do with Catherine's reaction to this story, which David has written by hand in the simple *cahiers* used by French schoolchildren. A disaster then occurs which is the worst that can befall a writer as a writer, and the ménage breaks up forever, two to stay together and one to leave.

—

At first reading this is a surprising story to receive from the great outdoor athlete of American literature. He has not previously presented himself as a clinician of bedroom practices. Even more interesting is the passivity of his writer hero, who, on the evidence, hates big-game hunting, and who is portrayed as totally subject to the powers of women, hapless before temptation, and unable to take action in the face of adversity. The story is told from David Bourne's masculine point of view, in the intimate, or pseudo, third person Hemingway preferred, but its major achievement is Catherine Bourne. There has not before been a female character who so dominates a Hemingway narrative. Catherine in fact may be the most impressive woman character in Hemingway's work, more substantive and dimensional than Pilar in *For Whom the Bell Tolls* or Brett Ashley in *The Sun Also Rises*. Even though she is launched from the naïve premise that sexual fantasizing is a form of madness, she takes on the stature of the self-tortured Faustian and is portrayed as a brilliant woman trapped into a vicarious participation in someone else's creativity. She represents the most informed and delicate reading Hemingway has given to any woman.

For Catherine Bourne alone, this book will be read avidly. But there are additional things to make a reader happy. For considerable portions of the narrative, the dialogue is in tension, which cannot be said of *Across the River and into the Trees*, his late novel of the same period, for which he looted some of the motifs of this work. And there are passages that show the old man writing with the strength of his early work—a description of David Bourne catching a bass in the canal at Le Grau-du-Roi, for example, or swimming off the beach at La Napoule. In these cases the strategy of using landscape to evoke moral states brings victory.

But to be able to list the discrete excellences of a book is to say also that it falls short of realization. The other woman and third main character, Marita, does not have the weight to account for her willingness to move in on a marriage and lend herself to its disruption. She is colorless and largely inarticulated. David Bourne's passivity goes unexamined by the author, except as it may be a function of his profession. But the sad truth is that his writing, which we see in the elephant story, does not exonerate him: it is bad Hemingway, a threadbare working of the theme of a boy's initiation rites that suggests, to its own great disadvantage, Faulkner's story on the same theme, "The Bear."

In David's character resides the ultimate deadness of the piece. His incapability in dealing with the crisis of his relationship does not mesh with his consummate self-assurance in handling the waiters, maids, and hoteliers of Europe who, in this book as in Hemingway's others, come forward to supply the food and drink, the corkscrews and ice cubes and fishing rods his young American colonists require. In fact, so often does David Bourne perform his cultivated eating and drinking that a reader is depressed enough to wonder if Hemingway's real achievement in the early great novels was that of a travel writer who taught a provincial American audience what dishes to order, what drinks to prefer, and how to deal with the European servant class. There are moments here when we feel we are not in France or Spain but in the provisional state of Yuppiedom. A reader is given to conclude that this shrewdest of writers made an uncharacteristic mistake in not finding a war to destroy his lovers, or some action beside their own lovemaking to threaten their survival. The tone of solemn self-attention in this

work rises to a portentousness that the seventy thousand words of
text cannot justify.

But here we are led back to the issue of editing a great writer's
work after his death. As far as it is possible to tell from biography,
and from the inventory of Hemingway manuscripts by Philip
Young and Charles W. Mann, Hemingway intended *The Garden of
Eden* as a major work. At one point he conceived of it as one of a
trilogy of books in which the sea figured. Certainly its title suggests
a governing theme of his creative life, the loss of paradise, the ex-
pulsion from the garden, which controls *The Sun Also Rises* and *A
Farewell to Arms*, among other books and stories. Apparently there
is extant more than one manuscript version for scholars to choose
from. Carlos Baker mentions the presence of another married couple in one of the versions, a painter named Nick and his wife,
Barbara. Of the same generation as David and Catherine Bourne,
Nick (is Adams his last name?) and Barbara live in Paris. And there
may be additional characters. Presumably, the material involving
them is in a less finished state and easily stripped away to find the
spare, if skimpy, novel we have now in print. But the truth about
editing the work of a dead writer in such circumstances is that you
can only cut to affirm his strengths, to reiterate the strategies of
style for which he is known; whereas he himself may have been
writing to transcend them. This cannot be the book Hemingway
envisioned at the most ambitious moments of his struggle to realize
it, a struggle that occupied him intermittently for perhaps fifteen
years. And it should have been published for what it is, a piece of
something, part of a design.

For there are clear signs here of something exciting going on, the
enlargement of a writer's mind toward compassion, toward a less
defensive construal of reality. The key is the character of Catherine
Bourne. She is in behavior a direct descendant of Mrs. Macomber,
of "The Short Happy Life," or of Frances Clyne, Robert Cohn's
emasculating lover in *The Sun Also Rises*, the kind of woman the
author has before only detested and condemned. But here she has
grown to suggest in Hemingway the rudiments of feminist perspec-

tive. And as for David Bourne, he is unmistakably the younger literary brother of Jake Barnes, the newspaperman wounded to impotence in that first expatriate novel. But David's passivity is not physical and therefore more difficult to put across. He reminds us a bit, actually, of Robert Cohn, whom Jake Barnes despised for suffering quietly the belittling remarks of women in public. Perhaps Hemingway is learning to dispense his judgments more thoughtfully. Or perhaps David Bourne was not designed as the hero of the piece at all.

—

With a large cast and perhaps multiple points of view, something else might have been intended than what we have, a revised view of the lost generation perhaps, some additional reading of a kind of American life *ex patria*, with the larger context that would earn the tone of the book. There are enough clues here to suggest the unmistakable signs of a recycling of Hemingway's first materials toward less romance and less literary bigotry and greater truth. That is exciting because it gives evidence, despite his celebrity, despite his Nobel, despite the torments of his own physical self-punishment, of a writer still developing. Those same writing strategies Hemingway formulated to such triumph in his early work came to entrap him in the later. You can see this beginning to happen in his 1940 novel *For Whom the Bell Tolls*, where implanting the conception of the book in geography and fixing all its action in time and relentlessly understating the sentences were finally dramatic strategies not formally sufficient to the subject. I would like to think that as he began *The Garden of Eden*, his very next novel after that war work, he realized this and wanted to retool, to remake himself. That he would fail is almost not the point—but that he would have tried, which is the true bravery of a writer, requiring more courage than facing down an elephant charge with a .303 Mannlicher.

(1986)

ORWELL'S 1984

Here is the story of one of the most widely read novels of our time.

The year is 1984. The globe is divided into three superstates—Oceania, Eurasia, and Eastasia. The war among them is constant and never-ending. However, the sympathies of the war change all the time. The people of Oceania sometimes find that Eurasia is the enemy and Eastasia the ally, and sometimes just the opposite. When Oceania's allegiances shift, everyone is made to forget that the circumstances were ever different. The public record is rewritten.

Winston Smith, a minor government employee of Oceania, is one of the thousands who are charged with rewriting history. He spends his days altering news stories, magazine articles, and other printed materials so that they'll conform to the propaganda demands of the government. The agency he works for is called the Ministry of Truth. In like fashion, the Ministry of Love is responsible for the torture and elimination of dissidents. And the Ministry of Peace is responsible for waging the never-ending war.

Oceania's head of state is a mustached, Stalinoid personage known as Big Brother. He is never seen in person, but his portrait is displayed everywhere—on billboards and in public squares—usually underscored with the words BIG BROTHER IS WATCHING YOU.

Winston's troubles with Big Brother stem from the day he wanders into a junk shop in a slum quarter of his city and buys an old blank diary. He begins to record his dissatisfactions. He writes out of the sight lines of the two-way telescreen in his apartment. There is no law against keeping a diary, but if he is found out, he will be executed or sent to a forced-labor camp for twenty-five years.

His troubles are only beginning. He notices a young woman colleague in his office who gives him surreptitious signs of her attraction to him. Her name is Julia. He works through his suspicions of Julia and meets her in a secluded glen in the countryside, where at least there are no telescreens, though there may very well be hidden microphones.

Winston and Julia become lovers, a treasonable offense punishable by death, inasmuch as Big Brother does not permit sex between unmarried partners and, in fact, condones it in married partners only for the purpose of procreation. Confronted with the problem of how to meet Julia on a regular basis without being detected, Winston goes back to the shop where he purchased his diary and rents a pied-à-terre over the shop, a charming room furnished, as in the ancient days before the great atomic wars, with a soft bed, curtains, a fireplace, and antique bric-a-brac. The lovers take to going there when they can steal the time from their bleak existence. They make love, sleep, and read the secret manifesto of the subversive revolutionary organization known as The Brotherhood, to which they've decided to give their allegiance.

But, as it happens, the idyllic room is monitored by a hidden telescreen. The antiques shop and the pied-à-terre are an artful construction of the Thought Police. Winston and Julia are arrested and taken to the dread Ministry of Love.

Winston's chief torturer is a high official named O'Brien, whom Winston thought to be a member of the revolutionary Brotherhood. In fact, O'Brien gave him the secret manifesto. Under O'Brien's tutelage, he is beaten, questioned, and electrically tormented for a period of months until all the rebellion is expunged from him and he is able to agree, with tears of love in his eyes for his torturers, that two and two are five. What breaks him finally is the threat of the worst punishment imaginable, the torture in "Room 101," where such as he are simply exposed to what they fear most—in Winston's case, rats. As a rat cage is about to be strapped to his face, he begs O'Brien to inflict this torture on Julia instead, thus destroying his last bit of self-respect and moral integrity.

In the final scene of the book, Winston sits in an outdoor café, reclaimed, rehabilitated, totally broken, and gazing with adoration at the enormous face on the screen in the public square. "He loved Big Brother," says George Orwell, the author of this tale, by way of an epitaph for his hero.

———

Even in synopsis, it is clear that *Nineteen Eighty-four* is an incredibly masochistic novel. The chief attribute of the hero is helplessness. The chief characteristic of his antagonist, Big Brother, is absolute, unremitting power. The state personified as Big Brother allows no resistance whatsoever, not even in the privacy of the mind. Individualism is a crime. Thought is a crime. Certainly, justice is out of the question, an obsolete concept. The hope of revolution is denied, because the revolutionary Brotherhood is probably a fiction. But even the personal consolations are withheld. Not only is love a capital offense. Not only is the natural world bugged with microphones. There is nothing to wear except uniforms. There is nothing to drink except a vile synthetic gin. There is nothing for the eye to see except an industrial landscape adorned with the staring face of the despot.

Compare the fate of Winston Smith with those of the traditionally beset heroes of English literature and you begin to appreciate the depths of Orwell's prophecy. Consider Dickens's novels of impoverished, scorned, mistreated orphan boys, the lowest of the low: By pluck, or luck, they find their patrimony, their true love, their middle-class ease. Shakespeare's errant kings go to their doom in the majesty of battle or madness. Ending well or badly, boys or kings put up a struggle; their lives have moral dimension. Orwell claimed his novel was political satire. But the heroes of classic satires, such as Gulliver and Candide, return safely home and find consolation from the weirdness or the evil of the world around them. They separate from their experience and are left whole by their authors. Orwell's satire leaves his hero without dignity, without mind, without a separate moral stature, either tragic or comic. We may be tempted to find in the life of Winston Smith a vision of original sin, except that among all the other things Oceania does without, it does without God.

Masochistic or not, *1984* has been in print continuously since publication. Its American paperback edition has had sixty-three printings. It is a work assigned to high school students as frequently as *Huckleberry Finn* or *The Call of the Wild*. What makes its success even more interesting—this grim, joyless book with its helpless hero and hopeless outcome—is that Orwell wrote it from the desire to instruct. Is there a straighter route to literary oblivion? After all, readers are likely to avoid a writer whose characters are less important to him than the ideas he wants to illustrate, who can't quite integrate into the action all the information he has to impart, who gives away the ending of his story in the beginning, and, worst of all, who writes to save mankind. *Nineteen Eighty-four* met all those requirements for disastrous publication.

Orwell's biographer Bernard Crick tells us that when the English publisher Frederick Warburg read the manuscript, he wrote, in a memo to his staff, "It is a great book, but I pray I may be spared from reading another like it for years to come." That goes to the heart of the matter. Who cannot be relieved to put the book down? But, as it happens, state sadism and individual helplessness characterize our century. Perhaps the millions of readers willing to endure Orwell's relentless despair find compensation in the totality of all his understanding—the way he puts it all in place, the daily confrontation of corrupted ideologies, the death and sanctimony that dazzle us each morning in newspapers, deafen us each night on the TV news.

—

Orwell's real name was Eric Blair. He was born in 1903 and was sent away at a young age to an English prep school called Saint Cyprian's. There his ordinary miseries of status as the son of comparatively poor parents were compounded by a bed-wetting problem, canings by the school's authorities, awful food, inadequate heat in winter, greasy public-bath water in which he had to immerse himself, and other torments. In such a setting there was no shortage of upper-form boys willing to bully the younger students, which suggests to some critics of *1984* that the Big Brother state is a metaphor for the awful childhood of young Master Blair. But it is not unusual for critics to avoid dealing with the substantive challenge of a book by referring to its author's life. Orwell's early work as a novelist was clearly autobiographical, and had he wanted to write a novel about Saint Cyprian's, he would have. In fact, he wrote a great essay on the subject titled "Such, Such Were the Joys." He was a modest, plain-spoken man not given to ridiculous aggrandizements of his own experience, and the idea of turning the whole world into a totalitarian nightmare because of an unhappy time in a boys' school would have seemed to him absurd.

Besides which, Orwell's entire life, not just his childhood, was difficult. As a young man, he worked in Burma as a British Imperial policeman (writing about the experience in his novel *Burmese Days*) and went back to Europe to live in terrible poverty as a free-lance writer (the basis for his novel *Down and Out in Paris and London*). He had turned politically leftward, and when the Spanish civil war began, he joined an international brigade, saw action, and received a throat wound from a sniper's bullet. His account of his experiences in Spain can be found in his dazzling work of reportage *Homage to Catalonia*. As a member of the Loyalist coalition fighting the Spanish Fascists led by General Franco, he underwent the crucial political revelation that the Communists, who were his nominal allies, were, from their own intense doctrinal self-interest, enemies of the Loyalist cause. He realized that at least one element fighting the Fascists was itself fascist. And from that insight and from what he learned of Stalin's purges and show trials, he derived his concept of totalitarianism as an extent of state power that renders irrelevant the ideology that has produced it.

That was not an easy lesson to learn in the thirties. Everyone on the left could see and deplore what fascism was quite clearly, but a leftist intellectual on the side of the workingman and against the cruelties of private wealth who could also see the errant energy of a left revolution as it was betraying itself was ahead of his time. Orwell's fate put him squarely inside the world of the twentieth century. It was his genius to see it for what it was. By the time of World War II, he was in London working for the BBC, still a socialist and writing "England Your England," an essay in praise of the solidarity of the English class structure he was committed, in principle, to change. It begins "As I write, highly civilized human beings are flying overhead trying to kill me." He would not for any cause render anything less complex or paradoxical than it was.

For many years, Orwell had suffered from tuberculosis. By the time he began to write *1984*, his condition was incurable and terminal. He was then forty-two, and what he had seen and thought and written had raised his aesthetic imagination to a visionary level. He had lived hard in the world, all over the world, and the world was what he wanted to talk about. He had lived in the trenches, walked bread lines, instructed himself in the matter of German concentration camps and Russian labor camps. He had seen what the United States had done with its atom bombs. The cold war had begun, with its accelerating arms race. Orwell composed *1984* as a work of political satire, a judgment of the world he lived in by a prophecy of what it was in danger of becoming. Transpose the numerals of his year of darkness and you get 1948, the year in which the book was finished.

—

But the exquisite torment of authorship is that no book, no matter how great, can legislate the way in which it is to be read. In the

United States, intellectual cold warriors read *1984* as only a warning against Soviet communism. In the popular press, it was not infrequently seen as an attack on the idea of socialism generally and, by association, on liberals who were less than steadfast in their ideological defense of the free-enterprise system.

More or less in vain did Orwell issue a statement through his publisher that his book was not a simple prophecy of what would happen if we let down our guard against communism ("Specifically the danger lies in the structure imposed on socialist and liberal capitalist communities by the necessity to prepare for total war with the U.S.S.R. . . ."). Nevertheless he had written a convenient and useful text for the early days of the cold war. Poor Orwell, a democratic socialist to the day he died, was acclaimed in England by the Tories and in America by the right-wing professional anti-Communists, ex-Communist spies, confessors, repenters, and FBI men then publishing Communist-under-the-bed warnings every day in the week and ready to raise the only real writer among them, they thought, to their shoulders.

Still, it may have been ingenuous of him to expect otherwise. The surface of the book glitters with descriptions of life derived in balanced measure from Nazi Germany and Soviet Russia. Daily the Oceanians are convened at work or on the streets for a ritual called the Two Minutes' Hate, an orgy of mindless rage directed at whichever of the other superstates, Eurasia or Eastasia, happens to be the enemy of the moment; but more often against The Brotherhood and its leader, a formerly loyal party leader named Immanuel Goldstein. The Two Minutes' Hate recalls Hitler's use of the German media for the frenzied production of hyperpatriotic, racist events by which every appalling excess of his government was justified and every military adventure ennobled. At the same time, the figure of Goldstein is portrayed with an unmistakable resemblance to that of Trotsky, and since Big Brother is described as looking like Stalin, the Soviet reference is substantial. Big Brother's ubiquitous portrait mirrors the personality cult of Stalin, with its giant banners, posters, murals, busts, which showed up everywhere in Russia—in every parade, on every wall, in every park. One thinks, too, of the degree of surveillance under Big Brother, the concept of *thought-crime*—punishable offenses not of action but of attitude—as having a Russian resonance; not just since the Revolution but for hundreds of years under the czars, the Russian secret police have generated a culture of paranoia.

The idea of corrective interrogation, enforced confession, is pointedly Communist—the Fascists simply beat people up and killed them. On the other hand, quite clearly a Nazi inspiration are the children in *1984*—vicious little sneaks and spies who turn their parents in to the secret police, just as children were encouraged to do in the Third Reich.

And so on. The careless reader who didn't see beyond the landscape of the book wouldn't understand just what moral was being drawn. The story Orwell tells is not of good nations against bad nations but of governments against individuals. Statism is rampant in 1984. The action is set not in Russia but in the Anglo-American superstate of Oceania. And what has turned life so grim and brought about the monstrous subjugation and degradation of Oceania's citizens is unending and unnecessary war. Living in a perpetual and artificial emergency, the citizenry cannot resist the Spartan militarization of life or the rigorously punitive means by which the government achieves national consensus. The greatness of *1984* comes not from its observations of dictatorships of the thirties and forties but from its vision of the totalitarianism implicit in the structure of the entire postwar industrial world.

—

The reader going back to the book after many years may be surprised to find what it is that commands most of the author's attention. Not the furnishings of the malign state—the police, the telescreens, the torture devices, the famous Room 101. What Orwell comes back to again and again all through the book is the idea of the political manipulation of reality through the control of history and language. Does that sound abstract, overintellectual? Consider yourself in a situation in which you see something on the street: A man is hit over the head, thrown into a car, and driven away. Suppose, further, that he is a man known to you and to others—a famous man. But none of the other people on the street will talk to you about what you and, presumably, they have seen. You are ignored. And when you go home to see if there is any report about the incident on the TV evening news, there is none. Nor is there any account of the matter the next morning in the newspaper. Suppose you are a brave or a persevering sort and you know where this famous man's residence is. You go there to tell the family what has happened. The house is unoccupied, the rooms are empty and no name is on the mailbox or the front door. The janitor tells you that no such person has ever lived there. You go to the police station and are told there is no record of that name in the census. Finally, you go to the library—the man was famous, after all—and discover no reference to him in any publication, registry or book. He doesn't exist and never did.

Winston Smith's job, remember, is to alter history. He changes facts and figures on command; he eliminates journalistic references to people who have been murdered; at one point, he even invents a fictitious person to make sense of an earlier deletion of another person from a Big Brother speech. And, until he himself is swept away, he is one of thousands who do that sort of work for the Ministry of Truth. "Do you realize," Winston says, trying to explain to Julia the terrible significance of such work, "that the past, starting from yesterday, has actually been abolished? If it survives anywhere, it's in a few solid objects with no words attached to them. . . . Every record has been destroyed or falsified, every book has been rewritten, every picture has been repainted . . . every date has been altered. And that process is continuing day by day, minute by minute. History has stopped. Nothing exists except an endless present in which the Party is always right."

Orwell's sensitivity to the political control of language is equally acute. One extremely important function of the Ministry of Truth is to prepare the "definitive Eleventh Edition" of the dictionary of

Newspeak. Newspeak is the official language of Oceania. It is being formulated to eventually replace Oldspeak, which is English. Why? Not only "to provide a medium of expression for the world view and mental habits" of the population but to "make all other modes of thought impossible." One of Winston's colleagues in the Ministry of Truth who is working on the dictionary explains the beauty of Newspeak:

> You think, I dare say, that our chief job is inventing new words. But not a bit of it! We're destroying words—scores of them, hundreds of them, every day. We're cutting the language down to the bone. . . . It's a beautiful thing, the destruction of words. . . . Take *good*, for instance. If you have a word like *good*, what need is there for a word like *bad*? *Ungood* will do just as well. . . . You haven't a real appreciation of Newspeak, Winston. In the end, we shall make thoughtcrime literally impossible, because there will be no words in which to express it. . . . In fact, there will be no thought as we understand it now.

The diminishment of thought through the constriction of language is such a crucial element of the Orwellian vision that a separate essay titled "The Principles of Newspeak" is appended to the book. It purports to be written well after the year 2050, when Newspeak officially replaced Oldspeak. "In 1984," we are told, "the word *free* still existed in Newspeak but could only be used in such statements as 'This dog is free from lice.' . . . It could not be used in its old sense of 'politically free' or 'intellectually free,' since political and intellectual freedom no longer existed even as concepts and were therefore of necessity nameless." In 2050, the word *free* is gone.

There is more operating here than a writer's jealous love of his native tongue. The falsification of history and the emasculation of language bring us to the center of the Orwellian nightmare. The ultimate totalitarianism is the absolute control of reality. It is far more frightening than Room 101. Orwell was a realist; he believed in a self-evidential, objective world of truth that is perceivable by the mind of man. But the book's heavy, O'Brien, Winston's articulate torturer, says to him, "Reality exists in the mind and nowhere else." And he proves it by conditioning Winston to believe, sincerely, that two and two are five. Orwell's obsessive return to this idea over and over again belies his confidence in objective reality. There is truth and it can be perceived, he seems to be saying, but only by the multiplicity of witness. Is he contradicting himself, committing a kind of *doublethink*? If truth is perishable, as he shows it to be in the world of 1984, then perhaps it is not self-evident and objective. In fact, under such totalitarian systems as exist in the world today, the effort of governments to command truth seems never-ending, as if it is not entirely possible. *Samizdat* copies of forbidden texts distributed secretly in the Soviet Union have created a new word whose meaning everyone in the world now understands. Dissidents not only in the Soviet Union but in various Fascist regimes in Latin America and elsewhere have learned the brave arts of the press conference in exile, the uses of international rights organizations, and so on, to press their claims for the truth of what is happening in their countries. And so the truth is objective and perishable simultaneously that depends for its expression on the bravery and sacrifice of a few stronger-than-average individuals.

Orwell is not a philosopher of knowledge, and the traditional philosophical problem of where reality originates—in the mind or outside in the physical world—does not, finally, interest him. What he is talking about is a state of experienceable horror in which the mind's volume is filled with authority and fear of punishment, the integrity of the moral soul is overthrown, and a person loses corroboration of what is happening to him, of what his life is, by reference to a past or by the educated articulation of the present. In the arguments Orwell gives to the torturer O'Brien, one is reminded of no other writer so much as Edgar Allan Poe. The characterological transformation of a human being lacking a history and a language is what Poe entertains as the experience of being buried alive, of being sealed up in a basement, brick by brick—perhaps having been lured there by an invidious promise—to scream your head off in the black, suffocating silence.

—

"Who controls the past," runs the Party slogan, "controls the future; who controls the present controls the past."

We may be tempted to agree with Orwell in principle but may not share his intensity of concern, feeling that as a writer of prophetic satire, he is given to exaggeration, except that some slight attention to stories current in the press on the eve of 1984 reveals that if anyone takes the composition of history and language as seriously as Orwell does, it is the people who run governments.

In Japan, recently, the minister of education decided that the history texts assigned to Japanese schoolchildren should be revised insofar as they referred to Japan's invasions and military occupations of China and Korea in the thirties. What had been referred to as Japanese "aggression" in those countries was changed to "advance," a more neutral military word that gave no indication of who was doing what to whom. In fact, even by twentieth-century standards, the atrocities committed by His Imperial Majesty's troops on the Asian mainland between 1937 and 1945 were noteworthy. The references to such atrocities have been glossed over. In addition, the uprisings of the conquered South Koreans against Japanese colonial rule of those days are now designated mere "riots" in the minister's revised texts.

Those are just the latest examples, according to a piece in *The Nation* by Donald Kirk, of a long-standing campaign by the Japanese government "not to dwell on old days," in the words of the education ministry, nor to allow attention to "extremely tragic subjects," such as the atomic bombing of Hiroshima and Nagasaki, but to see to it that publishers emphasize, under quaintly termed "guidance policies" set by the government, a respect for the patriotic mind, the family, and deference to the elderly—all of which sounds harmless enough, except that those were also the cultural values that dominated Japan during World War II, when it was an imperial terror in partnership with Nazi Germany. The new guidance policies come more or less simultaneously with two political developments: the rise of the right wing in the ruling Japanese Liberal Democratic Party (Orwell would relish the idea of a right-wing liberal democrat) and the year-by-year rise, with U.S. encouragement, of Japan's military budget—$11.5 billion annually as of last count—for its self-defense forces.

Japan is not a totalitarian state but a constitutional democracy.

Here's another example, closer to home. The U.S. Foreign Assistance Act specifies that for another country to qualify for our military aid, it must certifiably meet U.S. standards of human rights. *Human rights* is a term of great currency in our political language. When introduced, it tended to refer to a person's right to speak freely or to hold any political opinion of his choosing or to be tried swiftly and under due process of law in the event he was accused of a crime—in general, to any of the collective rights of Americans under the Constitution. But under pressure of worldwide practices, the term has taken on a humbler meaning. Now *human rights* refers to standards of treatment that you hope to expect of your oppressor after he has taken all your rights away. He should not pack you away in an isolation cell while denying publicly that you're under detention; he should not salt you away in a labor camp after a sentence by a kangaroo court; he should not on a whim machine-gun you in the street or hack you to death in your bed or with relish take you to a ditch and break every bone in your body before killing you. If you're an infant, you have the right not to have your skull smashed against a wall; if a nursing mother, not to have your breasts sliced off; if a nun, not to be raped and disemboweled; if an old man, not to be made to defecate in front of a crowd and eat your own excrement; if a boy or a young man, not to be castrated and have your severed organs stuffed into your mouth. The right not to have those things done to you—the right not to be tortured, mutilated, enslaved, or injudiciously murdered—is what we've come to mean by the term *human rights*.

In July 1982, in order to keep military aid flowing to the government of El Salvador, the Reagan administration certified to Congress that that government was making "substantial progress" in human rights. Yet, according to Thomas Sheehan, writing in the *Los Angeles Times*, offices of the archdiocese of San Salvador recorded, just in the first four months of the year, 2,334 political murders committed by "government forces or right-wing death squads, which are often composed of off-duty policemen."

Clearly, to advance its diplomatic and strategic interests, the Reagan government is willing to regard those political murders and atrocities as different in kind from the 84,000 civilian deaths previously attributed to the Salvadoran state forces. Somehow, those 2,334 murdered souls are harbingers of gentler times. Orwell, in his essay "Politics and the English Language," says, "In our time, political speech and writing are largely the defense of the indefensible." To defend the indefensible, you have to deform the language, use words not to communicate thought but to prevent it. You have to remake history. So the peasants and priests and nuns, the farmers and teachers and doctors and nurses and union leaders and schoolchildren who have been shot and hacked to death are "rebel elements." The desperate coalition in El Salvador of all political points of view but the ruling extreme right's is deemed a "Communist threat." A historical awakening, through the Catholic Church, of the perennially abused and disenfranchised peasantry is portrayed as a conspiracy of terrorists funded by the Soviet Union and administered by Cuba.

All over the world today, not just in the totalitarian countries, assiduous functionaries in Ministries of Truth are clubbing history dumb and rendering language insensible. And insofar as the above examples are concerned, it does not do to say that both we and the Japanese people have, at least, the means of corrective response— an alerted citizenry, a free press, opposition political parties, and so on. The population of a democracy can be only sporadically sensitive to historical lies. The opposition parties often endorse them. And a good percentage of the press is inclined by ownership to affirm rather than challenge political orthodoxy. Besides which, even in a democracy, the power of initiative belongs to the government. The effort required to check and redress crimes against truth is greater than the effort needed to commit them. Our massive involvement in Vietnam required only President Johnson's authorship of the Gulf of Tonkin Resolution. It took an aroused youth movement, a cultural revolution, a polarized society, ten years of mass marches on Washington, and 57,692 American dead and thousands more wounded to undo that one.

Of all the activities of an administration, its foreign policy is the least constrained by our system of checks and balances. More to the point, what President Reagan is doing in El Salvador has the inertial force of thirty-five years of cold war, the weight of enormous military and weapons-manufacture lobbies, the malign energy of premises that have not been seriously disputed or even questioned by any president since the death of Franklin Roosevelt in 1945. What this president is doing in El Salvador is consistent with what previous presidents have done in Chile, Vietnam, the Dominican Republic, Guatemala, and Iran. Three and a half decades of government-controlled reality, however resisted, cannot have left the national mind of our people undamaged; it is, after all, essentially corrupting to insist on carrying forward the ideals of democracy by denying its blessings to others. That is the world of doublethink, which Orwell describes as "to know and not to know, to be conscious of complete truthfulness while telling carefully constructed lies, to hold simultaneously two opinions . . . knowing them to be contradictory and believing both of them."

—

Big Brother brainwashes his subjects, rewrites their history and deadens their language, but his broadest means of control is the waging of war, or of what passes for war.

In 1984, says Orwell, the three superstates have long since had their nuclear war and stopped it short of total disaster because the end of organized society would mean the end of their power. They do, however, continue to develop and stockpile nuclear weapons in the hope someday of discovering a weapon of such unequivocal advantage that it "will kill several million people in a few seconds without giving warning beforehand." In the meantime, "propping each other up like three sheaves of corn," they fight a continuous nonnuclear war on the far borders of their territories. Each of them —they are roughly equivalent to the Anglo-American bloc, the Russian-European bloc, and the Chinese bloc—has everything it needs to sustain itself, which means that there is no need for war as in the old days, when nations fought for natural resources or markets or cheap labor. But since war goods do not add to a nation's real wealth, being useless for anything but war, the unending conflict serves the purpose of consuming the wealth of each of the great states without raising appreciably the standard of living of its masses. That is desirable because the real wealth of the world must be contained if the masses are not to become too comfortable and therefore too intelligent, for then they will no longer be willing to endure the injustices of a hierarchical society.

The continuous war also monopolizes public emotion, generates public fervor, and justifies encroachment on the private, individual mind. The war of superstates is therefore an "imposture," says Orwell. The real war is "waged by each ruling group against its own subjects, and the object of the war is not to make or prevent conquests of territory but to keep the structure of society intact."

This is satire, of course, but less so than it was when Orwell wrote the book.

—

How far are we, then, from realizing the prophecy of 1984?

If nuclear war breaks out, Orwell may be proved wrong that it will be a limited war, but if so, nobody will be alive to care. If he is right, we are hardly able to take comfort, given the postwar society he describes. What we have now, on the eve of the Orwellian year of judgment, are two coincident reality systems: the human reality of feeling and thought, life and love and death; and the suprahuman, statist reality of contending political-myth structures that would, in our name and from the most barbaric impulses, disenfranchise 99 percent of the world's population from even tragic participation in their fate. Inasmuch as no human being is god enough to grant to himself the disposition of nuclear weapons, and the destructive endowment of even one bomb transcends the limits of responsible human action, it will be the second system, the statist reality, that will get things going. The necessary abandonment of human values and the obliteration of logic and meaning by the ruler who engages a nuclear war ensure that the only surviving reality will be that of the political myth. And that is the heart of Orwell's prophecy. The state-managed death of individualism will have begun. Everyone will love Big Brother. The liberal, enlightened society with its claims of human entitlement—including life, liberty, and the pursuit of happiness—will be history.

Then it will not even be that.

(1984)

RONALD REAGAN

R onald Reagan was born on 1911 in rural Illinois. His father, John Edward Reagan, was a store clerk and erstwhile merchant whose jobs took the family to such towns as Galesburg, Monmouth, and Dixon—just the sort of places responsible for one of the raging themes of American literature, the soul-murdering complacency of our provinces, without which the careers of Edwin Arlington Robinson, Sherwood Anderson, Sinclair Lewis, and Willa Cather, to name just a few, would never have found glory. The best and brightest fled all our Galesburgs and Dixons, if they could, but the candidate was not among them.

The Reagans were a poor, close, hardworking family. With his older brother, Neil, Reagan sold homemade popcorn at high school football games and was charged with the serious business of maintaining the family vegetable garden. For many summers he worked as a lifeguard at Lowell Park on the Rock River in Dixon, pulling seventy-seven people out of the water by his own count and socking away most of his salary to make up college tuition.

The candidate attended Eureka College in Eureka, Illinois. He was no student. He had a photographic memory, and it was this trait, rather than application to books or innate cleverness, that got him through his exams. What really interested him was making the football team, pledging a fraternity, debating, and acting in campus theatricals. But his priorities were correct. Eureka, a fifth-rate college, provided meager academic credentials to its graduates. But a third-rate student at a fifth-rate college could learn from the stage, the debating platform, the gridiron, and the fraternity party the styles of manliness and verbal sincerity that would stand him in good stead, when the time came to make his mark in the world. In fact, the easy, garrulous charm Reagan developed at Eureka got results very quickly. Graduating in the depths of the Depression, he had no trouble finding a job as a radio announcer.

—

We have these facts from a biography, *The Rise of Ronald Reagan*, by Bill Boyarsky, a California journalist, and from the candidate's autobiography, *Where's the Rest of Me?*, the title of which is taken from his most memorable line as a film actor. In the picture *King's Row*, he played the role of a young rake who is careless with his attentions to the daughter of a surgeon; when he lands in the hospital after a car accident, the vengeful surgeon amputates his legs. Reagan delivers the memorable line coming to after the operation.

It was when he became a sportscaster for WHO in Des Moines that Reagan's peculiar affinity for simulated life began to emerge. He was called on to describe baseball games played by the Chicago White Sox and the Cubs on the basis of Western Union messages from the ballpark. These were characteristically brief—a hit, a walk, and so on—but the chatty Reagan made an art of describing the game he was not seeing as if he were sitting in the stands, with only a sound-effects man—crack of the bat, crowd cheers—to help him. He became quite popular with the regional audience and did promotional work on the side as the station's celebrity speaker, giving talks to fraternal lodges, boys' clubs, and the like, telling sports stories and deriving from them YMCA sorts of morals.

In 1937, Reagan went to Santa Catalina Island to cover the Chicago Cubs in spring training. The proximity to Hollywood reawoke his collegiate ambition to act, and he managed to get himself a screen test. He didn't really expect anything to come of it but was offered a contract by Warner Brothers for two hundred dollars a week. An agent had persuaded the studio that he was another Robert Taylor. Considering that actor's negligible store of animation, one can wonder now at the inducement. In any event, the candidate acted in more than twenty B-pictures before his big break came. In 1940, he persuaded Jack Warner to give him the role of George Gipp, the doomed Notre Dame football hero, in *Knute Rockne, All American,* a film about the famous football coach. His means of persuasion was a photograph of himself in his Eureka College jersey and helmet.

Subsequently, he was sanctified to play the role of a pubescent Shirley Temple's first screen beau in *That Hagen Girl.* There is no evidence that between takes they exchanged Republican philosophies. Thereafter his career ascended to such heights as the aforementioned *King's Row, The Voice of the Turtle,* and *The Hasty Heart;* descended to the likes of *Bedtime for Bonzo,* in which the lead was a chimpanzee; and sank forever in *Hellcats of the Navy,* a black-and-white 1950s film about submarines. All in all, Reagan acted in close to fifty movies over a twenty-year period and the relevance of this achievement to a presidential candidacy should not go unexamined.

With few exceptions, film stars in the 1930s and 1940s lived in a peculiar state of public celebrity and private humiliation. It was the primary condition of their fame that their worth was constantly under question. The studios had a lock on everyone and actors were punished and rewarded and otherwise dealt with as children by the paternalistic film moguls who held their contracts. Stars were property. In most cases their personal lives were as closely directed as their film lives. How and with whom they conducted themselves were the responsibilities of publicity departments. Their names were changed, and plastic surgeons improved their faces. All in all, they lived in that meld of life and typecasting we call stardom but which was often, in fact, self-obliteration.

Films were made then as they are today, not by actors but by producers, directors, and technicians. The working life of the stars was tedium—waiting for the technicians to get around to them, doing scenes in no reasonable order, more often than not repeating them to the point of distraction. No sane adult could long take pride in this sort of mannequin work. Actors bloomed and faded, destroyed themselves in scandal, drugs, and drink, gave themselves to public rebellion, or cultivated a rampant narcissism. A few even tried to produce and direct their own films. It is instructive that Ronald Reagan resorted to none of these stratagems of protest and self-expression. He seemed to agree with assessments of his talents as modest. He did not burningly aspire to serious acting. He followed the rules of the game, was easygoing and cooperative, made friends of influential gossip columnists and producers, sought contacts, and acted generally the good boy, perceiving through the endless reaches of this devastatingly hollow life one salient fact: it was a good living. Perhaps if his talent had been greater or his need to accomplish something really worthwhile had been stronger he wouldn't have lasted as long as he did.

At the beginning of World War II, Reagan, a reserve second lieutenant in the cavalry, was called up for active duty. Here, presumably, was the occasion for reality to make its intrusive claims on the life of a professional fantasist. But he was assigned to the First Motion Picture Unit of the Army Air Corps and spent the war at the Hal Roach studio in Culver City. He narrated training films, one of the most notable being *Target Tokyo*. Saipan-based B-29 superfortress pilots preparing to firebomb Japanese war plants in Ota were shown—by means of special effects, miniature topography, and traveling shots made from a moving crane—how the ground below would appear as they made their bombing run.

Only after the war did Reagan's life begin to attach to the nonfictive structure of things. He became active in the Screen Actors Guild and after a time was elected its president. Of course it was not exactly a blue-collar union that had on its rolls Gary Cooper, Spencer Tracy, future Republican senator George Murphy, and Republican presidential TV adviser Robert Montgomery. Nevertheless, this was the postwar period of tough jurisdictional disputes between movie craft unions, one reputedly led by gangsters, and it was also the time when the House Un-American Activities Committee began to ask movie stars their opinions of the international godless Communist conspiracy. The candidate got a behind-the-scenes view of some rough politics. He seemed to like it well enough, testifying before the HUAC and taking a militantly square-jawed stand on these matters of national urgency with the same kind of midwestern good-boy appeal that was later to attract the attention of some conservative Californians looking around for a gubernatorial candidate in the 1960s.

The odd thing, though, was that while Reagan was devoting more and more time to being spokesman for the Screen Actors Guild, his career as an actor was going into decline. Paradoxically, he was getting more press and prestige as a union officer than as an actor. It is generally believed that this period of his life marked the transition from actor to politician. But in effect he was becoming an actor figure, a front for working actors, and though his activities were now clearly in the realm of the real, if insane, world, the personal quotient of pretense was still high. He was a union official pretending to be a successful movie star.

It was in this Pirandelloesque state of being that he married a fairly obscure MGM contract player named Nancy Davis. The circumstances that brought them together are worth noting. The daughter of an ultraconservative Chicago surgeon, Miss Davis became concerned when she began to receive mail from left-wing organizations in the early 1950s. She consulted the director Mervyn LeRoy, who suggested that they bring the problem to the attention of guild president Reagan. This seemed to Miss Davis a splendid idea—apparently she was happy to have any pretext to meet the handsome actor. The director phoned Reagan, who consulted union membership files, found that Miss Davis's name had been confused with that of another actress, and gave her a clean bill of health. LeRoy, unlikely Cupid though he was, suggested that Reagan bring the good news personally to Miss Davis by taking her out to dinner. Reagan complied, and it was in this manner, after giving her a loyalty check, that Ronald Reagan met his wife-to-be.

The final formative period in the candidate's history of self-realization is the eight years or so he spent as the face and voice of the General Electric Company, selling its products and benign motives to the American public on television. He introduced the weekly stories of the *G.E. Theater* and gave the sales pitch. But that wasn't all. When he was not on camera he went around to the G.E. plants, shaking hands with the assembly-line workers and giving speeches at middle-management luncheons. The chief executives of G.E. were at this time concerned about employee morale—not job security or better pay but a smile and a handshake from a movie star was their formula for improving it. In truth, it was this period and not his tenure as a union official that manifested the political content of the candidate's life and passion. He began to perfect a speech, the same speech he would give as a national politician, with ever-changing topical references and gags to keep it fresh, in which all the nostalgia for his midwestern boyhood—the ideals of self-reliance, hard work, belief in God, family, and flag—came into symbolic focus in the corporate logo hanging like a knight's coat of arms behind the dais.

Particularly, his tenure as G.E. spokesman overlapped the years in which the great electrical industry price-fixing scandal was going on. While Reagan extolled the virtues of free enterprise in front of the logo, G.E., along with Westinghouse, Allis-Chalmers, and other giant corporations, was habitually controlling the market by clandestine price-fixing and bid-rigging agreements, all of which led, in 1960, to grand jury indictments, in what was characterized by the Justice Department as the largest criminal case ever brought under the Sherman Anti-Trust Act. Three G.E. executives pleaded guilty and went to jail. The company was fined, and some people to this day think Ralph Cordiner, the chairman of the board, himself narrowly escaped prosecution. Reagan, of course, was totally innocent of all of this, and there is no indication his innocence was ever shaken by the news.

Even now, as the Republican candidate for the presidency, he would probably be shocked if it was suggested to him that these days the Horatio Alger hero is a multinational corporation. William Safire quotes him as saying that he doesn't want to use the word "ideology" in his speeches because the American people think it's a "scare word." More likely he doesn't think he should be unfairly tagged with having one. The pictures of him in the newspapers as often as not show him in his prewar pompadour, smiling somewhat quizzically at age sixty-nine, as if not quite understanding why others don't perceive the rational, logical, inevitable, but above all descriptive American truth of his politics.

The journalists who have studied his years as governor of California find Reagan's record was not all that bad—surprisingly moderate in many areas, and certainly within the normal range of the politics of compromise, the give-and-take between executive and legislative branches that keeps most governments of this country, state as well as federal, in centrist balance. That may be encouraging to some, but of all his previous job experiences, as sportscaster of invisible ball games, studio actor, Culver City commando, television salesman, the governorship of California probably has least relevance to his presidential candidacy. His own accounts of what he did in California are charmingly demagogic, as though he is seeking to prove that he was more conservative in office than he is given credit for. Some reports have it that he did not act like a governor, that he went home at five o'clock in the afternoon and forgot the job until the next morning. He scrupulously kept his private life private—very odd in the American political tradition, where one's spouse, children, parents, sisters and brothers, medical problems, and psychological difficulties are all grist for the mill. The impression is that he turned his governor's persona on and off with a ventriloquial indifference.

The candidate has chosen not to travel abroad in the only available time before the campaign begins in earnest because he doesn't want to give his opponents the chance to accuse him of trying to acquire instant expertise in his weak department, foreign policy.

Always image-conscious, he has not thought, nor, apparently, have his advisers, that by going abroad he might possibly learn something.

In any event, the nomination is his who has pursued it giving pep talks and doing dinners and shaking hands and smiling and raising money and speaking simplistic fantasy for most of his adult life. One could write of the people behind Ronald Reagan, but that is another story. He has beaten the best the Republican primaries have had to offer—senators and governors, cabinet officials, congressmen—and the party that honored us with Richard Nixon will now offer him. Ladies and gentlemen, I give you the next president of the United States.

(1980)

COMMENCEMENT

D r. Handler, members of the board of trustees, deans of the
university, honored doctoral recipients, distinguished members of the faculty, parents, friends, and most especially the pride
and point of these proceedings, the shining, resplendent Class of
1989:

Good morning, class. You've been going to school all your lives,
and in a few minutes you'll be free. But not until I've finished
talking to you. I'm the last compulsory lecture of your undergraduate careers. I represent your faculty's last shot at you, their last
chance to tell you what they meant, before you slip out of their
grasp forever.

You know, a few miles away, not one but two heads of state are
this moment about to address graduates like yourselves in a stadium seating thirty thousand people. [President George Bush and
François Mitterrand were attending the Boston University commencement exercises nearby.] What they say will be of only theo-
retical interest to the young men and women somewhere in that
crowd whom they are presumably there to address. Perhaps they
will use the occasion to enunciate major foreign policy statements,
and when they are through, they will get back into their motor-
cades with the Secret Service men running alongside, and lift off in
their helicopters, and the TV cameras will shut down, and the army

of reporters will scatter, and those students, at least the ones who didn't scalp their graduation tickets, will be able to look at one another and say, "Well, it is historic to see a president, but what, after all, has been celebrated here?"

What, indeed?

It seems to me that your university this morning looks very, very good by way of contrast. Your president and faculty and board of trustees have presumed a commencement should be directed to the graduating seniors in an academic setting that retains its meaning and integrity, that what is being celebrated is the moment of your personal rite of passage, the moment of the beginning of your post-collegiate lives. And they know it's a crucial moment, a solemn celebratory moment, that should not be scanted; and so I'm honored to be called upon to speak to you, not a politician but a writer, a novelist included, I like to think, among the "unacknowledged legislators of the world," in Shelley's phrase—you English majors know that—unacknowledged like the poets, like the artists, in fact, helpless legislators of created consciousness who from the struggles of their own minds make poems and stories that would contribute to the moral consciousness of their time.

So I will begin by turning for instruction to an earlier unacknowledged legislator, a story writer, a novelist, who lived and flourished in the 1920s. His name was Sherwood Anderson, and he's most famous today for a small book of stories about life in a small town in middle America around the turn of the century. *Winesburg, Ohio* is the title of this book. Some of you may know it. And in his introduction to the book, Anderson proposes a theory which he calls the theory of grotesques. It is not a scientific theory but a historical poetic theory of what happens to people sometimes as they strive to give value and meaning to their lives.

Here is the theory: that all about us in the world are many truths to live by, and they are all beautiful—the truth of patriotism, the truth of self-reliance, and so on. But as people come along and try to make something of themselves, they snatch up a truth and make it their own predominating truth, to the exclusion of all others. And what happens, says Anderson, is that the moment a person does this, clutches one truth too tightly, the truth so embraced becomes a lie and the person turns into a grotesque.

Suppose, for instance, you're thrifty and you work hard and scrimp and save and live modestly in order to pay your way through college. Your thrift is a good thing. But then afterward, in later life, long after it is necessary, you continue to deny yourself and you save and save until hoarding money becomes an end in itself. Your thrift has become a lie. You've turned into a miser. You've become a grotesque. You see how it works? If, for instance, your patriotism blinds you to all other moral and ethical truths, and from your love of country you deceive duly constituted bodies of governmental authority, and you break laws and shred documents, the truth of patriotism has turned to a lie in your embrace of it, and made you a grotesque. Or take the truth of self-reliance. It is undeniably beautiful. It was the truth that underlay the entire administration of the previous president, Ronald Reagan: this idea of self-reliance, rugged individualism. Who wouldn't like to stand up for himself, independently, and make his own way through life? Yet Mr. Reagan's advocacy of self-reliance caused him to scorn or forget other truths—of community, for example, and the moral responsibility we have toward those with fewer advantages, and the profound truth of the interdependence of all society's citizens. And so he was moved at various times in his administration to take away school lunches from needy children and tuition loans from students, and to deny legal services to poor people and psychological counseling to Vietnam veterans, and Social Security payments to handicapped people. You see how it works, this theory?

In fact, I will venture to say that insofar as Mr. Reagan inserted his particular truth into the national American mind he made it the lobotomizing pin of conservative philosophy that has governed us and is continuing to govern us at this very moment.

The philosophical conservative is someone willing to pay the price of other people's suffering for his principles. And so we now have hundreds of thousands, perhaps millions, of our citizens lying around in the streets of our cities, sleeping in doorways, begging with Styrofoam cups. We didn't have a class of permanent beggars in this country, in the United States of America, fifteen or twenty years ago. We didn't have kids selling crack in their grade schools, or businessmen magnifying their fortunes into megafortunes by stock manipulation and thievery. I don't remember such epidemics of major corporate fraud. A decade ago you did not have college students scrawling racial epithets or anti-Semitic graffiti on the room doors of their fellow students. You did not have cops strangling teenage boys to death or shooting elderly deranged women in their own homes. You did not have scientists falsifying the results of experiments, or preachers committing the sins against which they so thunderously preached. A generation or so back you didn't have every class of society, and every occupation, widely, ruggedly practicing its own characteristic form of crime.

So something poisonous has been set loose in the last several years as we have enjoyed life under the power and principles of political conservatism. And I have used Sherwood Anderson's theory of the grotesque to account for it, but I don't know what to call it: a gangsterdom of spirit, perhaps. I do know that to describe it is bad form. To speak of a loss of cohesion in society, a loss of moral acuity, is tiresome. It is the tiresome talk of liberalism. In fact, part of this poisonous thing that I'm trying to describe is its characteristic way of dealing with criticism: It used to be enough to brand a critic as a radical or a leftist to make people turn away. Now we need only to call him a liberal. Soon "moderate" will be the M word, "conservative" will be the C word, and only fascists will be in the mainstream. And that degradation of discourse, that, too, is part of this something that is really rotten in America right now.

Some of you, perhaps some of your parents, may be wondering at this time if I am speaking appropriately for this occasion, which is, after all, a celebration. In answer, I have to say I believe my subject is all too appropriate; I think it is my obligation to tell you, as truthfully as I can, the context, the social setting in which you will find yourself when you walk out of here with your degree. As an unacknowledged legislator, I am giving you not a State of the Union address but a State of the Mind of the Union address.

What does it do to you young people, I wonder, to grow up in a time in which the bottom-line standard of business thinking now controls every aspect of our lives? You may have heard our president ask just the other day that the Senate delay its consideration of a bill to apply stricter ethical standards to government officials. Mr. Bush is worried that if men and women are made to behave honestly, they won't want to work for his administration. That's funny, except that at one time people were honored to be called upon to use their expertise for the sake of their country. There was an ideal of public service, and financial sacrifice was part of that ideal. Now, it is taken for granted by everyone in Washington that people can be expected to come to work for their country only if they can afterward turn a trick from it.

It is in this context that I find myself thinking of a lately deceased Brandeis graduate, as unbusinesslike a person as you'd ever meet. He is not the sort of alumnus you would expect to be mentioned or that I would expect to mention in a commencement address. His name was Abbie Hoffman. Class of '59. I knew Abbie, though we were not close, and I didn't have that much contact with him after the sixties. The truth is I found him easier to take from a distance; I have to admit that our ways were different, but I admired him tremendously. He was fearless, and very funny, with the humor, the precision of insight, of a great political cartoonist. And as an activist he put his body on the line. In the sixties he was a scruffy sort of fellow, skinny and nimble, somewhat unwashed-looking with his torn T-shirts and jeans, his long hair, his headband. He was a founder of the Yippies, the Youth International Party. And he was in the vanguard of the antiwar movement in the days of big street demonstrations, much like the one they have been having in China, the students, these days, and for the same reasons, to bring government into alignment with the popular will of the people.

Anyway, Abbie did street theater; he staged events that might be clownish or vulgar but that invariably caught the attention of the media and enraged the authorities. (For instance, I remember he once wore a shirt made from an American flag, and when angry policemen tore it off his back he shouted, "I have only one shirt to give for my country!") He got people terribly mad, Abbie, and for very good reason: He was insufferable. He was insufferable because he held the mirror up so that we saw ourselves. That's just what the biblical prophets did, they operated in just that way. Wasn't it Isaiah who walked abroad naked to prophesy the deportation of the Jews? And wasn't it Jeremiah who wore a yoke around his neck to prophesy their slavery? Same insufferable thing. So Abbie was a kind of unacknowledged legislator of this order. Once he organized a demonstration to ring the Pentagon and by means of prayers and incantations make it rise from the ground and levitate. And another thing he did, he stood in the gallery overlooking the New York Stock Exchange and threw handfuls of dollar bills down on the floor and watched all the traders scramble to pick up the money. These were prophetic acts, were they not? Throwing money onto the floor of the Stock Exchange knowing people would crawl around in a frenzy to pick it up? The Pentagon and the Stock Exchange are in the eighties the twin images of our idolatry. He had it exactly right.

It's my view that in the last decade or so of life in our country, roughly the time since you were in the tenth grade, we have seen a national regression to the robber-baronial thinking of the nineteenth century. This amounts to nothing less than a deconstruction of America, the dismantling of enlightened social legislation that had begun to bring equity over half a century to the lives of working people, to rectify some of the terrible imbalance of racial injustice and give a fair shake to the outsiders, the underdogs, the newcomers. We have seen the ideals of environmental sanctity sacrificed to the bottom-line demands of business thinking in which we have done only as much to protect our environment as industry has found convenient, as if only a few songbirds and some poor dumb animals were at stake, as if the bleeding hearts of woodsy environmentalists were the issue, and not our lungs and skins and genes, and the wholeness and health of our children and their children. We have seen a new generation of nativist know-nothings called up like primitive comic-book warriors to make overt the covert racism and anti-Semitism of the campaign demagoguery of our conservative politicians. And we have seen with more and more deadening frequency the banning of the books of our heritage in our schools and public libraries, as for instance in Panama City, Florida, where they have found it necessary to expunge such dangers to the republic as *Wuthering Heights, Hamlet, The Red Badge of Courage,* and *The Autobiography of Benjamin Franklin.*

So that we may in fact have broken down, as a social contract, in our time, as if we were supposed to be not a just nation but a confederacy of stupid murderous gluttons.

So that, finally, our country itself, the idea, the virtue, the truth of America, is in danger of becoming grotesque.

This is certainly serious stuff for a happy day, but I would not be doing honor to you and to this occasion if I did not tell you what's been going on while we've been waiting for you.

That is something else I meant to say. That we've been waiting for you. Did you know that? Your mothers and fathers and grandmothers and grandfathers, in fact all the generations older than yours, have been watching you and waiting for you. Because whether you know it or not, you have learned here at Brandeis the difference between authentic thought and cant, between rational thought, honest perception, on the one hand, and simplistic intellectual flummery on the other. And that makes you very precious to us, and to our nation.

And if your teachers here have seemed to you at various times to possess commanding intellectual presence, and I trust they have, the truth is they are itinerants, like you, having given their lives over to the strange species-grooming that is peculiarly Homo sapient: the modest, exhausted instruction in mind-survival of the generations that will succeed theirs.

And everything impractical they've given you, lines of poetry, phrases of music, and philosophical propositions, and ancient histories, and myths and dance steps, is terribly practical, in fact, the only means we have of defending the borders of a magnanimous, humanist civilization—just that civilization which is today under such assault.

The presumption of your life here, the basic presumption, is that every life has a theme. It is a literary idea, the great root discovery of narrative literature: every life has a theme and there is human freedom to find it, to create it, to make it victorious. And so however you find your society as you walk out of here, you do not have to embrace its lies, or become complicitors to its cruelties. Perhaps that is what your faculty wanted to say to you.

You are in charge of yourselves.

The stack of books you've collected in your four years here is an icon of the humanist ideal.

You have sanctity of thought, the means to stay in touch with the truth.

Your living, inquiring, and lighted minds are enlisted in the struggle for a human future and a society unbesieged by the grotesqueries of stupidity and terror.

Yes, I think that's what your faculty might want me to tell you.

You may not have realized it, and we are somewhat embarrassed to have to say it, but willy-nilly and ipso facto, you commence this day in the name of civilization.

I have every confidence in you. And I congratulate you. From up here I have to say you all look beautiful to me. Your families, I know, are proud of you, your teachers are proud of you, Brandeis University is proud of you, and let me say as an itinerant speechmaker, I find that I am proud of you too. God bless you all.

(1989)

THE CHARACTER
OF PRESIDENTS

M r. Bush has said, by way of defaming Mr. Clinton's character, that the character of a presidential candidate is important. So it is. The president we get is the country we get. With each new president the nation is conformed spiritually. He is the artificer of our malleable national soul. He proposes not only the laws but the kinds of lawlessness that govern our lives and invoke our responses. The people he appoints are cast in his image. The trouble they get into, and get us into, is his characteristic trouble. Finally, the media amplify his character into our moral weather report. He becomes the face of our sky, the conditions that prevail. One four-year term may find us at reasonable peace with one another, working things out, and the next, trampling on each other for our scraps of bread.

That a president is inevitably put forward and elected by the forces of established wealth and power means usually that he will be indentured by the time he reaches office. But in fact he is the freest of men if he will have the courage to think so and, at least theoretically, could be so transported by the millions of people who have endorsed his candidacy as to want to do the best for them. He might come to solemn appreciation of the vote we cast, in all our multicolored and multigendered millions, as an act of trust, fingers crossed, a kind of prayer.

Not that it's worked out that way. In 1968 Richard Nixon re-bounded from his defeat at the hands of Jack Kennedy, and there he was again, his head sunk between the hunched shoulders of his three-button suit and his arms raised in victory, the exacted re-venge of the pod people. That someone so rigid and lacking in honor or moral distinction of any kind, someone so stiff with crip-pling hatreds, so spiritually dysfunctional, out of touch with every-thing in life that is joyful and fervently beautiful and blessed, with no discernible reverence in him for human life, and certainly with never a hope of wisdom, but living only by pure politics, as if it were some colorless blood substitute in his veins—that this being could lurchingly stumble up from his own wretched career and use history and the two-party system to elect himself president is, I suppose, a gloriously perverse justification of our democratic form of government.

I think of the president's men cast in Mr. Nixon's character: con-victs-to-be Ehrlichman, Haldeman, and Mitchell; and Henry Kis-singer, who seemed to go through the ranks as if magnetized, until he stood at the president's side, his moral clone in the practice of malefic self-promotion. I think of the events sprung from Mr. Nixon's character: the four students going down in a volley of gun-fire in the campus park of Kent State University. More than seven thousand antiwar marchers detained in a stadium in Washington, D.C. The secret bombing of Cambodia, the secret deaths, the secret numbers, the always secret realpolitik operations. And one other lingers in the mind: the time he ordered plumed golden helmets, Bismarckian tunics, and black riding boots for the White House honor guard.

The subsequent two holders of the office, Mr. Ford and Mr. Carter, showed hardly any character at all, the one a kind of stolid mangler of the language whose major contribution to American history was to pardon Richard Nixon, the other a well-meaning but terribly vacillating permanent-pressed piety who ran as a liberal and governed as a conservative. We jogged in place during their terms of office. Nobody in America can remember where they were during Mr. Carter's term, or what they were doing, or if they had any waking life at all. Mr. Carter's biblical fundamentalism gave him exceptional patience in the negotiation of a peace between Israel and Egypt, but Washington looked nothing like the Sinai and did not inspire him. The ancient Near East was his glory and, with the failed desert operation to rescue the hostages in Iran, his downfall. He did define human rights as a factor in international relations but did not become an honorable champion of the idea until he had left office. His vapidity is remembered, like the nervous smiles flitting across his face, as an invitation to the electorate to bring in the wolves of the right who had all this time been pacing back and forth and fitfully baying in the darkness beyond the campsite.

—

And so in 1980 we found ourselves living the mystery of Ronald Reagan.

With not much more than his chuckles and shrugs and grins and little jokes, Mr. Reagan managed in two elections to persuade a majority of the white working/middle class to vote against their own interests. The old self-caricaturing B-movie actor had the amazing capacity to destroy people's lives without losing their loyalty. He was said to go blank without a script, and his political opponents could think of nothing worse to call him than, in the words of Clark Clifford, an "amiable dunce." But his heartfelt pieties and simplistic reductions of thought, his misquotations and exaggerations, his mawkish appeals to rugged self-reliance, spearheaded a devastating assault on the remedial legislation that had been enacted from the New Deal to the Great Society, set off new brazen white-racist furies across the land, and culminated in the most dangerous conspiracy against American constitutional government in the twentieth century.

The old deaf actor who nodded off in staff meetings managed always to wake up in time to approve schemes at variance with his oath of office. He refused to enforce civil rights laws, subverted the antitrust statues, withheld Social Security payments from disabled people, cut off school lunches for needy children, and gave into private hands the conduct of American foreign policy in Central America. Under the persona of this fervent charmer, we were released into our great decade of deregulated thievery, and learned that the paramount issues of our age were abortion and school prayer. Meanwhile, the rich got filthy rich, the middle class turned poor, the profession of begging for alms was restored to the streets, and the national debt rose to about $3 trillion.

Now there was a president with character.

—

Since the end of the war in Vietnam, American government under Republican presidents has been punitive. Their philosophy is called conservatism, but the result in these many years of its application has been to dissipate the wealth of the country and lower the standard of living, health, and the hopes of an education of all but the top economic stratum of society. That is punitive. What Mr. Clinton refers to, inadequately, as the trickle-down theory is really the oligarchical presumption that no one but an executive citizenry of CEOs, money managers, and the rich and well-born really matters. When Mr. Reagan talked of getting "the government off our backs" what he meant was freeing this executive from burdens of public polity. No regulatory agency must stand in the way of our cutting timber, no judge can enjoin us from acting to restrain the competition, no labor law must stop us from moving a manufacturing plant to Indonesia, where they work for a tenth of the wage. For that matter, women will have no legal rights in the conduct of their own personal lives, and the fate of all citizens, as well as the natural world they live in, or what's left of it, is to be entrusted perpetually to the beneficent rule of the white male businessman to whom God in His infinite wisdom has given the property interests of the country.

There is an electoral strategy for implementing this nineteenth-century baronialism, and we are seeing and hearing it again in this campaign because it has always been very effective. It relies on the mordant truth that the right-wing politician has less of a distance to go to find and exploit our tribal fears and hatreds than his opponent who would track down and engage our better selves. That it seeks out and fires the antediluvian circuits of our brains is the right's advantage in every election. Pat Buchanan at the Republican convention was the Neanderthal baring his canines and waving his club.

The right will always invoke an enemy within. They will insist on a distinction between real Americans and those who say they are but aren't. This latter group is your basic nativist amalgam of people of the wrong color, recent immigration, or incorrect religious persuasion. At the beginning of the cold war "fellow travelers" and "pinkos" were added to the list (Communists being historically beyond the pale). Mr. Nixon contributed "effete intellectuals"; Mr. Reagan's secretary of the interior, James Watt, threw "cripples" into the pot with Jews and blacks; and this president and his men have consigned to perdition single parents, gays and lesbians, and a "cultural elite," by which they mean not only the college-educated, cosmopolitan (Jewish and their fellow-traveling) residents of both coasts who write or work in publishing, films, or television but really any person in any region of the country who is articulate enough to compose a sentence telling them what a disgrace they are.

Mr. Clinton's dissenting actions during the Vietnam War place him at the head of the dark and threatening coalition of faux Americans. He is, finally, the treacherous son who dares to oppose the father. As far as Mr. Bush and his backers are concerned, when the young people of this country rejected the war in Vietnam, they gave up their generational right of succession to primacy and power. They could no longer be trusted. Neither could the democracy that spawned them, like an overly permissive parent, ever again be trusted.

All the presidents since Vietnam, from Nixon to Bush, have been of the same World War II generation. They will not be moved. The thrust of their government has been, punitively, to teach us the error of our ways, to put things back to the time when people stayed in their place and owed their souls to the company store.

In June 1989 Mr. Bush vetoed a bill that would have raised the minimum wage to $4.55 an hour over three years. In October 1989 he vetoed a bill that included a provision for the use of Medicaid funds to pay for abortions for poor women who were the victims of rape or incest. In October 1990 he vetoed the Civil Rights Act enacted by Congress to set aside Supreme Court rulings that make it more difficult for women and minorities to win employment-discrimination suits. In October of the next year he vetoed a bill extending benefits to people who had exhausted their twenty-six weeks of unemployment insurance (reversing himself in November to sign a more modest extension). On June 23 of this year he vetoed a bill that would have allowed the use of aborted fetuses in federally funded research. In September he vetoed the family leave bill, which would have entitled workers to unpaid time off for births or medical emergencies in their families. In July he vetoed the "motor voter" bill, which would have allowed citizens to register to vote when applying for driver's licenses.

The would-be beneficiaries of these bills—people who sweep floors, kids who work at McDonald's, poor women, blacks, the critically ill, people who've lost their jobs, working mothers and fathers, and nonvoters (can't have too many of those)—always heard from Mr. Bush at the time of the veto that they had his sympathy, but that somehow, or someway, the bills on their behalf would not have done what they were designed to do and in fact would have made their lives worse.

Mr. Bush is a man who lies. Senator Dole, who ran against him in 1988, was the first to tell us that. Vice President Bush lied about his opponents in the primaries, and he lied about Mr. Dukakis in the election. President Bush lies today about the bills he vetoes, as he lies about his involvement in the arms-for-hostages trade with Iran and continues to lie, even though he has been directly contradicted by two former secretaries in the Reagan Cabinet—Shultz and Weinberger—and a former staff member of the National Security Council. He lies about what he did in the past and about why he is doing what he is doing in the present. He speaks for civil rights but blocks legislation that would relieve racial inequities. He speaks for the environment but opposes measures to slow its despoliation.

You and I can lie about our actions and misrepresent the actions of others; we can piously pretend to principles we don't believe in; we can whine and blame others for the wrong that we do. We can think only of ourselves and our own and be brutally indifferent to the needs of everyone else. We can manipulate people, call them names, con them and rob them blind. Our virtuosity is inexhaustible, as would be expected of a race of Original Sinners, and without doubt we will all have our Maker to answer to. But as to a calculus of damage done, the devastation left behind, the person who holds the most powerful political office in the world and does these things and acts in these ways is multiplied in his moral failure to a number beyond the imagining of the rest of us.

Nevertheless, there is something hopeful to be discerned in all of this. Mr. Bush is a candidate on the defensive. His term in office has been disastrous. This presidential heir to the conservative legacy of Mr. Nixon and Mr. Reagan has about him the ambience of the weak dauphin. His own right-wing constituency is disgusted with him, possibly because he portends the end of an age, the decadence of a ruling idea, or merely the played-out vein of the Republican gold mine. Certainly he is, in all his ways, less than resolute. Lying is a tacit admission of having done something inadmissible. A mosaic of presidential lies offers the cryptic image of a better world.

All else being equal, what sort of presidential character is most likely to take us there?

Who would not wish for someone, first of all, who realizes that once elected, he cannot be the president merely of the constituency that empowered him but, if he would fill the defining role of the office, must be a president on behalf of everyone? That is a simple grade-school concept and, given the relation in America of money to politics, cannot be anything more than that. But the president who had the courage to live by it would immediately lead a reformist movement to erase the advantages big money accords to itself by its political contributions and its lobbying. This would presume a morally intelligent president as well as a courageous one.

I would wish for a developed historical sense in the president, one that could understand and honestly acknowledge that the political philosophy of what we lovingly call the free market has in the past justified slavery, child labor, the gunning down of strikers by state militias, and so forth.

I would want a presidential temperament keen with a love of justice and with the capacity to recognize the honor of humble and troubled people. And the character of mind to understand that even the borders of the nation are too small for the presidential service—that willy-nilly and ipso facto we're planetary blunderers now.

The true president would have the strength to widen the range of current political discourse, and would love and revere language as the best means we have to close on reality. That implies a sensibility attuned to the immense moral consequence of every human life. Perhaps even a sense of tragedy that would not let him sleep the night through.

Also, I should think he would be someone who really likes children, who laughs to be around them, and who is ready to die for them—but who would never resort to the political expedient of saying so.

Perhaps Mr. Bush's major contribution to this campaign is his raising of the idea of character in the public mind. He cannot have thought it through: We've been living with him. We know his mettle. When a candidate is up for a second term we don't have to rely on his actions as a twenty-three-year-old graduate student at Oxford to determine if he's got the goods. But it may be finally a great service to the electorate, and even a personal redemption of sorts, that he invites us to imagine by contrast with his own and his predecessors' what the character of a true American president should be.

(1992)

The Beliefs of

Writers

All writers relish stories from the lives of the masters. We hold them in our minds as a kind of trade lore. We hope the biography of the great writer yields secrets of his achievement. As many writers as Hemingway inspired to write he probably inspired to hunt or to box. I imagine many of them crouching this very moment in their duck blinds. Writers always want to learn how to live as a means of bringing out the best they have in themselves.

The master's life I've been thinking about lately is Tolstoy's, in particular his crisis of conscience at the age of fifty. Always at the mercy either of his passions or his ethics, Tolstoy lived in a kind of alternating current of tormented resolution. The practice of fiction left him elated and terribly let down. It's said that he had to be prevented from throwing the finished manuscript of *Anna Karenina* into the fire. In any event, at the age of fifty he decided that his life lacked justification, that he was no better than a pander to people who had nothing better to do with their time than to read. And he gave up writing novels.

Of course, his resolve did not seem to cover the shorter form, and over the years he lapsed into the composition of a few modest pieces—"The Kreutzer Sonata," "The Death of Ivan Ilyich"—but for the most part he employed his position and his talents to militate against some of the overwhelming misery of life under the czar. He indulged a prophetic voice. He preached his doctrine of Christian nonviolence. He wrote primers designed to teach the children of peasants to read.

Now theoretically, at least, there is for every writer a point at which he or she might come to the same conclusion as Tolstoy, a point at which circumstantial reality overwhelms the very idea of art or seems to demand a practical benefit from it; when the level of perceived or felt communal suffering or danger makes the traditional practice of literature for traditional purposes intolerable. But even a casual examination of literary history finds a readier disposition for this crisis of faith in Europe, where the passion of art has often been a social passion. So in Russia we have not only the example of Count Tolstoy stomping around in his peasant boots but the young Dostoevsky and his circle arguing everything about fiction except its enormous importance to history and human salvation. And in France we have Sartre and Camus, among others, conceiving a response to the moral devastation of World War II, a literary Resistance that includes drama, allegory, metaphysics, and handing out pamphlets in the streets.

With certain exceptions, American writers have tended to be less fervent about the social value of art and therefore less vulnerable to crises of conscience. The spiritual problems of our writers are celebrated but of a different kind from those having to do with the problem of engagement. Our nineteenth-century masters lived in sparse populations. Forests, the sea, the prairie, were images of terrifying freedom. So we've been brought up on solitude as much as society. We have a different faith to lose. I think of the despair of Hemingway, for instance, which led him to turn one of his shotguns on himself, or Faulkner's and Fitzgerald's, which led them to drink themselves into ruin. The problem as they lived it was a torment of success or failure but in any event some recognition of mortal limits, some inconsolability of rugged individualism formulated entirely as a private faith. Tolstoy, we should remember, lived to write his last novel, *Resurrection*, when he was in his seventies.

His ego is no less colossal, but our American masters thought with theirs to hold up the earth and sky.

So in thinking about Leo Tolstoy's attitude, I'm very much aware of its foreignness. We have had one decade in our own literary history, the 1930s, when politics and art, engagement, seemed to be on everyone's mind, but we take this period as a time of misfired artistic energy, of duped intellectuals and bad proletarian novels. Having turned ideological, we suffered for it, or so the lesson goes. American novelists since then have tended to cast themselves resolutely as private citizens and independent entrepreneurs. There is certainly no tradition among us for serving our country as senators and ambassadors, as our European and Latin American colleagues do. Our ancestry reveals an occasional customs inspector. We see the public value of our work as an accident of its private diction. Our attitude is expressed succinctly by the naturalized American poet W. H. Auden, who said a writer's politics are more of a danger to him than his cupidity. We worry that if a work is formed by ideas exterior to it, if there is some sort of programmed intention, a set of truths to be illustrated, the work will be compromised and we'll produce not art but polemic. We want our novels pure. We dislike about *War and Peace* that Tolstoy lectures us on history. He was always that way, we think, not just after the age of fifty.

Oddly enough, the aesthetic piety just described places the artist's idea of himself centrally in the American heartland. The notion that we are the independent entrepreneurs of ourselves is a national heritage. Irving Howe, among others, has pointed out that working people in the United States, unlike their European counterparts, refuse to identify themselves as a class. They tend to define themselves not by their work but by what they own from their work, the property they've accumulated, their ethnic background, their social activities—by anything, in short, that points up their distinction from the larger community. For the independent entrepreneur of himself, there is upward mobility, at least across generations, and there is the road— he can hit the road when things go bad, pull up stakes, move on. All this, including the writer's idea of what he can allow in his art and what he cannot, expresses our great operative myth of individualism.

We are thought as a country to be nonideological and nonsystematic in the way we go about conceptualizing our problems and solving them—or not solving them. We are chronically and by nature suspicious of systematic solutions. We're pragmatists. We like to go out in the barn of the Constitution and tinker. Writers no less than blue-collar people share the national aversion for the intellect, for the passion of the intellect, and the voices we find for our books are a shade more ironical and less epic than the Tolstoyan basso profundo. In preference to the Olympian view from the mountain we settle for the authority of the egalitarian witness, the pragmatic deposer of what he can confirm with his own eyes and ears.

If there was a moment when this piety of literary practice was set to harden, perhaps it was in 1940 with the publication of Hemingway's *For Whom the Bell Tolls*. What preceded it was a decade of intense debate carried on both within the work of novelists and critics and outside it in journals and in symposia or conferences. Almost no serious work of the era was not informed by the presumption of social crisis. Confronted with the miseries of the Depression, and the rise of the modern totalitarian state, writers and artists and intellectuals argued the alternatives to industrial capitalism. We are told this in Malcolm Cowley's book *And I Worked at the Writer's Trade*. The spirit shared inescapably by every American artist was the longing for ideal community. Among writers this spirit moved as much in the thought of conservative Southern Agrarians like John Crowe Ransom and Allen Tate, who could project a utopia based on the civilities of southern farm life; or T. S. Eliot, behind whose Waste Land lay a golden, God-lit medieval city; as in the more numerous prophets of the varieties of Marxian socialism.

And outside the books the value and justification of literature, of any art, came into furious debate. Whatever position a writer took, from formalism to communism, the need to take some position was inescapable. The writer's destiny was to be confronted with his conscience, to find his place, draw his lines. Commitment—to what? Engagement—of what sort? The process was both brutal and complicated. The world didn't stay still but moved along. History contaminated pure thoughts, the right causes got mixed up with the wrong people, ideals gave away to expediency, and hateful writers did good work and noble writers did lousy work. But everyone—good writers, bad writers—seemed to be in touch with what was going on in the world.

Hemingway himself had published a novel in 1937, *To Have and Have Not*, in which the Hemingway hero, a smuggler off the Florida coast, came as close as he ever had to articulating a communal sentiment. His name in this book is Harry Morgan and he's made to say "A man alone ain't got no bloody fucking chance." This is a monumental insight coming from the younger sibling of the romantically self-involved expatriates of the earlier novels.

Hemingway's next novel was to take place in Spain at the time of the civil war. He had seen the war firsthand; he was more worldly and more in touch with things than either Faulkner or Fitzgerald. Though he was a Loyalist, he deeply mistrusted and came to detest the Communists who ran things for the Loyalist side. This judgment, which turned out to be sound, was not unlike that of George Orwell in *Homage to Catalonia*. But it was Orwell, the European, who took what he learned to the point of revelation, the political prophecy of *1984*. We find by contrast in *For Whom the Bell Tolls* that a man alone may have no bloody fucking chance but it can be very beautiful that he hasn't. The Hemingway hero is now named Robert Jordan and he's a young American volunteer on the Loyalist side, a demolitions expert who is coming to the mountains to blow a bridge held by the Phalangists. He ends up dying alone, heroically, having taken over the leadership of the partisan band he's joined and sent them away to live on, his own code of honor the only enduring value of The Civil War of the Spanish people. The most international of American writers, was, morally speaking, an isolationist. War is the means by which one's cultivated individualism can be raised to the heroic. And therefore, never send to ask for whom the bell tolls; it tolls so that I can be me.

Now before you or I overread my claim, or what it is I'm getting to, let me take a moment to clarify something. I mean not to make pronouncements about literature but to speak of literary belief, which is something else than literature. Literary belief is the culture of presumptions and ideas that govern those of us who live our lives as writers. So I do not intend here to contrast Realism and Experimentalism or to speak of the Romantic tradition or the influences of Modernism or any of that sort of thing, which properly is the province of the literary critic and historian. What I'm doing is thinking out loud about where we are now, all of us, in our practice of fiction and perhaps how we got here. What do we believe about our writing, our calling, what do we think its possibilities are? In a catalogue of publications by the University of Chicago Press, I recently noticed a title that interested me, *The Soviet Novel: History as Ritual*, by Professor Katerina Clark. The copy advises that Professor Clark's study of the Soviet novel turns on the idea of its serving as a repository of official myths. Now that I know the fate of dissident Soviet authors and have met them in numbers in this country, this seems a reasonable claim and I look forward to reading the book. But I warrant that some of the serious works of American fiction, no less than our kitsch, in some ways serve as repositories for our myths, though of course not by direction and of course our myths are not official, at least not until recently. And a consideration of Hemingway now fifty or sixty years later has to include the possibility that his popularity with the public and among young writers was in part due to his service as a repository of American myth. The entrepreneurial self had come in for some rough treatment from Melville in *Moby-Dick* and from Dreiser in *Sister Carrie*. But Hemingway found its most romantic face. Withdrawal from society, distrust of it, despair of it, have been preponderant in our fiction ever since Robert Jordan withdrew from life and love and looked out over the barrel of his rifle on the last page of *For Whom the Bell Tolls*. It is as if given the self, nothing but the self—not God, not the state, love, or any conviction of a universal order—we have made ourselves its annotators. We may have rejected Hemingway's

romance—the self has become absurd, blackly humorous, and, finally, shattered and fragmentary—but, and this is the point, it is
ours.

Surely we can say of contemporary fiction without fear of contradiction that it suffers from a reduced authority, certainly for its
readers, who seem to be reading less of it. It may be that the most
avid readers of new fiction in America today are film producers, an
indication of the trouble we're in. But what is more peculiar is the
reduced authority of fiction in the minds of writers themselves,
who seem to want to take on less and less of the world with it. This
is an impression, of course, nothing more. And even as I test it in
my mind with several significant exceptions, it nevertheless seems
valid to say that there is a timidity to serious fiction now, some
modesty of conception and language, that has pulled us back from
its old haunts. There seems to be a disposition to accept some rule
largely hidden, to circumscribe our analysis and our geography, to
come indoors and lock the door and pull the shades and dwell in
some sort of unresounding private life.

Of course, fiction as traditionally practiced has always dealt with
private life. High seriousness in literature is attached to the belief in
the moral immensity of the single soul. If the artist is lucky or a
genius, the specific creation of his belief, Emma Bovary, Carrie
Meeber, Stephen Dedalus, Jay Gatsby, Joseph K., implicates the
universe. We become more who we are in the imposition on ourselves of these morally illuminating fictive lives. But of these characters I've listed, the books in which they find their animation make
society at large the antagonist, whether as middle-class provincialism, religious culture, or government bureaucracy; the fate of these
individuals issues from their contention with or concession to the
vast world around them. And the geography of the book is vast.
The heroine of *Sister Carrie* is, like her lover Hurstwood, a soul
dominated by the material lures of the big city. We witness her
sentimental education, not in the emotions of love, for which neither she nor anyone else in the book has endurance, but in the
emotion of social and economic advancement. There's no claim in

Dreiser for the consistent government of the human mind, exactly
the sentimentalism at the root of so many well-written, fashionably
ironic novels of private life done today. And so our awareness
moves out concentrically over Chicago, over New York, over the
whole United States. And then it keeps going.

It is that moving outward, that significant system of judgment,
that is missing in much of our work today. Of course, we have now
a considerable history of this reduced literature and of course it's
not exclusively American. An early retreat was sounded in the
1950s by Robbe-Grillet. But it's the American phenomenon I'm trying to understand and locate: an exhaustion of the hope that writing can change anything, or the discovery that all the wickedness is
known and thoroughly reported, that all the solutions to the wickedness are known, that nothing changes, it all goes on, with only
the freshness of expression lost, and the power of the art. Some sort
of raging, amoral system inside of which the artist is astute only in
the act of withdrawal.

There are many exceptions to this generalization, of course.
We've had novels about Vietnam. And certainly it is less true as
applied to black writers and to writers who are feminists. Yet it is
true for all of us that rather than making the culture, we now seem
to be made by it, even when we are being traditional novelists
reporting on what we see and making a morally comprehensive
world. Somehow in this postmodernist time we have been cowed.
We lack some rage of imagination, the imperial earth-shaking intention on the one hand, that—the world not responding properly—
would cause us to give up our writing altogether on the other. So
that, with Tolstoy, we would rail against art as we had before railed
against life.

And there's a corresponding drift among critics. I think of the
few works by my contemporaries that are examples of political
fiction. They only accentuate the prevailing rules. There is no poet-
ics yet devised by American critics that would treat engagement as
anything more than an understandable but nevertheless deplorable
breakdown of form. It is my impression, perhaps unjustified, that

for some segments of our critical community, the large examination of society within a story, the imposition in a novel of public matters on private life, the lighting of history within an individual, places a work in aesthetic jeopardy. Thus the social novel is seen always as ideological. In fact, if the subject of the novel is of a certain sort, if the novel is about a labor union organizer, for example, or a family on welfare, it is assumed to be political, that is, impure, as for example a novel about life in prep school is not. Political is always to be distinguished from what entertains. The CIA novels of William Buckley are thought to entertain. Whereas some months ago in *The New York Times Book Review,* a critic, Robert Alter, said of Joseph Heller's novel *Catch 22* and a novel of mine, *The Book of Daniel,* that they were flawed by a spirit adversarial to the Republic.

The final distinction is, of course, between political and literary, a quaint distinction and probably a source of amusement to writers in other parts of the world, Nadine Gordimer in South Africa, for example, or Milan Kundera of Czechoslovakia, Günter Grass of West Germany, García Márquez of Colombia, and it would have given a good laugh to Stendhal, Dickens, Dostoevsky, and Malraux. I think it is no slander to suggest that some of our critics are more likely to accept the political novel and even acclaim this or that example as long as it is written by a foreigner about a foreign country. This is analogous to President Reagan's support of workers' movements as long as they are in Poland.

Let's get back for just a moment to the 1930s. No one could seriously want the thirties to be held up as any kind of model age. There is nothing remotely desirable that I can see in Depressions or Crystal Nights or show trials. I don't imagine the purpose of history is to inspire art. I don't agree with Faulkner that "Ode to a Grecian Urn" is worth any number of old ladies—or old men. I don't think Faulkner is worth the antebellum South, and I would rather not have had Kafka at the price of twentieth-century European carnage. But in trying to locate contemporary American writing I look at the thirties, that supposedly meager decade of misfired artistic energy and of duped intellectuals and bad proletarian novels, and I see not just Faulkner and Hemingway and Fitzgerald and Thomas Wolfe but James T. Farrell, Katherine Anne Porter, Richard Wright, Nelson Algren, William Saroyan, John Steinbeck, John Dos Passos, Nathanael West, Dorothy Parker, Edward Dahlberg, Dalton Trumbo, Zora Neale Hurston, Horace McCoy, Erskine Caldwell, Lillian Hellman, James Agee, Edmund Wilson, Daniel Fuchs, Henry Roth, Henry Miller. For starters. A literature of immense variety and contention, an argument from every side, full of passion, excessive, self-consuming.

Literary life in the present is, by comparison, decorous. It's very quiet today. Is it because our society is sunlit and perfect? Are all our vampires staked through the heart? Or have we, as writers, given up our presumption of the authority of art, of the central place of the sustained narrative critique in the national argument?

Alfred Kazin has an idea about the thirties that might be appropriate here. "That crucial period," Kazin says, "turned out to be stronger in counter-revolution than in revolution, in the power of the state than in the apostolic freedom of the individual soul." He goes on to say, "Orthodoxy was becoming the norm in the '30s, not radicalism. The period that seems so easy to sentimentalize as one of struggle against poverty and oppression actually saw the triumph of Fascism in Germany and Spain, the unchecked dominion of Stalinist terror over what was radical in Communism itself. In this country the statism seemingly necessary for the crisis legislation of the New Deal was soon with Pearl Harbor to hammer out social regimentation and forms of intellectual control that many Americans now regard as the norm."

Of course, I'm taking his remarks out of context. But if Kazin is right—and listening to the shrill voices of conservatism in culture as well as everything else, how can we doubt it?—then we have some suggestion of the ultimate dependence of the artist upon the people he would speak for. And why not? We conceive the work of art as the ultimate act of individuation, but it may be seen also as a production of the community. Narrative is the art closest to the ordinary daily operation of the human mind. People find the meaning of their lives in the idea of sequence, in conflict, in metaphor, and in moral. People think and make judgments from a confidence of narrative. The narrative mode of thought comes naturally to everyone, as for instance mathematical or scientific reasoning does not. One imagines in the dawn of prehistoric human life that storytelling did not have to be invented as, say, counting or the wheel did. Everyone, all the time, is in the act of composition; our experience is an ongoing narrative within each of us. The novel duplicates the temporality of life and the authority for the telling of the novel is most often the death of its characters—the same authority, in the words of the great critic Walter Benjamin, "which even the poorest wretch in dying possesses for the living around him."

Thus, ironically, in our withdrawal, our nonpolitical pragmatic vision of ourselves and our calling, we writers may be expressing the general crisis of our age. We are writing as we live, in a kind of stunned submission to the political circumstances of our lives and the establishmentarian rule of our politicians. We are being bought off by our comforts while great moral outrages are committed in our name. A statist ideology encroaches on the realm of individual thought.

I would not mean to imply that the problems of writers under these circumstances are not the least of America's problems. But the coercion of realpolitik, the ideology of cold war, and the shadow of the bomb, may have robbed us of the passion of our calling, which is the belief that writing matters, that there is salvation in witness and moral assignment. These days many of our best writers do a kind of passive prophecy. They concentrate on the powerlessness or haplessness of our lives, and the inappropriateness of our public places for human life or the inadequacy of our culture for the conduct of human emotion. An inadvertent social critique comes off their pages without that level of rage that would drive them to and fro, like Leo Tolstoy, from art to the conviction that nothing is more important than teaching the children of the poor to read. The young writer today who picks up tonally, philosophically, on the Hemingway romance, is in danger of misperceiving the predominant condition of things, which is that the future for any of us is not individual. As independent entrepreneurs of ourselves with no control over our destiny, we may be failing the task. How will we be able to stay true to the changing nature of our lives if we hold to a myth that is being nullified by history? If our response to what is going on today were appropriate, it would probably produce books of a grubbier, sloppier, and more energetic sort than we are doing. Books with less polish and self-consciousness, but about the way power works in our society, who has it, and how it is making history. In order to begin to rebuild our sense of ourselves, we may have to go back to childhood, to the past, and down into our dreams, and start again. In order to reclaim our society, we need the words to find it. If we make that effort, everything I've been pondering here may be not an end but a beginning. And that should dilate your nostrils, young writers, and give you a scent of the chase.

(1985)

A Citizen Reads
the Constitution

N ot including the amendments, it is approximately five thousand words long—about the length of a short story. It is an enigmatically dry, unemotional piece of work, tolling off in its monotone the structures and functions of government, the conditions and obligations of office, the limitations of powers, the means for redressing crimes and conducting commerce. It makes itself the supreme law of the land. It concludes with instructions on how it can amend itself, and undertakes to pay all the debts incurred by the states under its indigent parent, the Articles of Confederation.

It is no more scintillating as reading than I remember it to have been in Mrs. Brundage's seventh-grade civics class at Joseph H. Wade Junior High School. It is five thousand words but reads like fifty thousand. It lacks high rhetoric and shows not a trace of wit, as you might expect, having been produced by a committee of lawyers. It uses none of the tropes of literature to create empathetic states in the mind of the reader. It does not mean to persuade. It abhors metaphor as nature abhors a vacuum.

One's first reaction upon reading it is to rush for relief to an earlier American document, as alive with passion and the juices of outrage as the work of any single artist:

We hold these truths to be self-evident, that all men are created equal, that they are endowed by their Creator with certain unalienable Rights, that among these are Life, Liberty and the pursuit of Happiness. That to secure these rights, Governments are instituted among Men, deriving their just powers from the consent of the governed. That whenever any Form of Government becomes destructive of these ends, it is the Right of the People to alter or to abolish it, and to institute new Government.

Here is the substantive diction of a single human mind—Thomas Jefferson's, as it happens—even as it speaks for all. It is engaged in the art of literary revolution, rewriting history, overthrowing divine claims to rule and genealogical hierarchies of human privilege as cruel frauds, defining human rights as universal, and distributing the source and power of government to the people governed. It is the radical voice of national liberation, combative prose lifting its musketry of self-evident truths and firing away.

What reader does not wish the Constitution could have been written out of something of the same spirit? Of course, we all know instinctively that it could not, that statute-writing in the hands of lawyers has its own demands, and those are presumably precision and clarity, which call for sentences bolted at all four corners with *wherein*'s and *whereunder*'s and *thereof*'s and *therein*'s and *notwithstanding the foregoing*'s.

Still and all, our understanding of the Constitution must come of an assessment of its character as a composition, and it would serve us to explore further why it is the way it is. Here is something of what I have learned of the circumstances under which it was written.

THE BACKGROUND

The Constitutional Convention was called in the first place because in the postwar world of North America influential men in the government, in the Continental Congress, were not confident that the loosely structured Articles of Confederation, as written, could make permanent the gains of the Revolution. Without the hated British to unite them the states would revert to bickering and mutual exploitation. They had as many problems with one another as the classes of people in each state had among themselves, and men like George Washington and James Madison foresaw a kind of anarchy ensuing that would lead to yet another despotism, either native or from foreign invasion by the Spanish or again by the English. Many competing interests were going unmediated. The agrarian Southern states, with their tropical rice and cotton plantations, saw danger to themselves in export taxes applied to all their goods by the North Atlantic port states. The small states, like Delaware, felt threatened by their bigger neighbors, such as Pennsylvania. There was immense debt as a result of the Revolution, which debtors wanted to pay off with state-issued paper money—and which creditors, security holders, bankers, merchants, men of wealth, wanted returned in hard currency. There were diverse ethnic and religious communities, black slaves, white indentured servants. And there were Indians in the woods. The states not contiguous had little in common with one another. To a New Yorker, South Carolina was not the South; it was another kingdom entirely, with people of completely different backgrounds and with bizarre manners in speech and deportment—foreigners, in short. Georgia and South Carolina depended on slave labor to run their plantations. Slavery was abhorrent to many Northerners in 1787, and an economy of slaves was morally detestable.

It is important to remind ourselves in this regard that colonial society had existed for one hundred and fifty years before the idea of independence caught on. That's a long time, certainly long enough for an indigenous class of great wealth to arise and a great schism to emerge between the rich and the poor. A very few people owned most of the land and were keenly resented. Three percent of the population controlled 50 percent of the wealth. People were not stupid; there was general knowledge of the plunder, legal chicanery, favoritism, privilege of name, and corruption of government officials that had created such inequity. In fact, it is possible that organization of public sentiment against King George is exactly what saved the colonies from tearing themselves apart with insurrections of the poor against the rich; that events like the Boston Tea Party and calls to arms by Jefferson and Tom Paine created the common enemy, the British, to unify all the classes in America and save, by diversion of anger and rage to the redcoats, the fortunes and hides of the American upper class. This was the class, as it happened, of most of the fifty-five men who convened in Philadelphia. Washington was perhaps the largest landowner in the country. Benjamin Franklin possessed a considerable fortune, and Madison owned several slave plantations.

There was an additional factor to make them sensitive. The convention had been called to consider amendments to the Articles of Confederation. The Continental Congress was even now sitting in New York City and doing government business, and not all that ineffectually. It was, for example, passing legislation outlawing slavery in the western territories. But rather than amending the Articles, the convention in Philadelphia was persuaded to throw them aside entirely and design something new—a federal entity that would incorporate the states. The agenda for this course of action was proposed by Governor Edmund Randolph of Virginia, who presented a number of resolutions for debate, and so it has come to be called the Virginia plan. But the sentiment for something new, a new federal government over and above state sovereignties, had the strong support of influential delegates from several venues. And so the convention got down to business that was actually subversive. It violated its own mandate and began to move in the direction the federalists pushed it. It was because of this and because no one participating wanted, in the vigorous debates that were to ensue over the next months, to be confronted with a record of his remarks or positions, that the conventioneers agreed to make their deliberations secret for the entire time they sat, permitting no official journal of the proceedings and swearing themselves to a press blackout, as it were. That was to upset Jefferson greatly, who was off in France as a minister; the idea of such secrecy repelled him. However, Madison, fortunately for us, kept a notebook, which did not come to light until 1843 but which provides us the fullest account of those secret deliberations and the character of the minds that conducted them.

THE CONVENTION

What a remarkable group of minds they were. The first thing they did was constitute themselves as a Committee of the Whole, which gave them the power of improvisation and debate, flexibility of action, so that when the collected resolutions were decided on they could present them to themselves in plenary session.

Methodically, treating one thorny question after another, they made their stately way through the agenda. If something could not be resolved it was tabled and the next issue was confronted. Nothing stopped their painstaking progress through the maze of ideas and resolutions from which they slowly constructed a new world for themselves: who would make the laws, who would execute them, who would review their judicial propriety; should the small states balk at proportional representation, then the Senate would be created to give equal representation to every state. Some matters were easy to agree on—the writ of habeas corpus, the precise nature of treason. If one reads any of the dramatic reconstructions of their work, and there are several good books that provide this, one has the thrill of watching living, fallible men composing the United States of America and producing its ruling concept of federalism, a system of national and local governments, each with defined powers and separate legal jurisdictions.

Through it all Washington sat up at the front of the room, and he never said a word. The less he said, the more his prestige grew. They had settled on one chief executive, to be called a president, and everyone knew who it would be. He had only to sit there to give the delegates courage to persevere. Franklin, too, lent the considerable weight of his presence, only occasionally saying a few soft words or passing up a note to be read by the speaker. Franklin was an old man at the time, over eighty. At one point, when the proceedings were bogging down in dissension, he offered the recommendation that everyone stop and pray. The lawyers were so stunned by this idea that tempers cooled, probably just as he had intended, and the meeting went on.

And as the weeks wore on there slowly emerged among the delegates—or must have—a rising sense of their identity not only as Carolinians or Virginians or New Yorkers but as American nationals. A continental vision of nationhood lit their minds, and a collaborative excitement had to have come over them as day after day, month after month, they fantasized together their nation on paper. One cannot read any account of their deliberations without understanding how they made things up as they went along from their own debated differences, so that a sort of group intellect arose. It was wise with a knowledge of the way men act with power and from what motives. This objectification of separate personalities and interests came of a unanimous familiarity with parliamentary method and was finally self-propelling. These men invented a country of language, and that language celebrated—whether in resolutions of moral triumph or moral failure—the idea of law. The idea of a dispassionate law ruling men, even those men who were to make and effect the law.

Enough resolutions having been put forth, a Committee of Detail was formed to get them into an orderly shape, and that was accomplished with the scheme of articles, and sections under the articles, grouping the resolutions about legislative, judicial, and executive branches, the rights and obligations of the states, the supremacy of the Constitution as law, etc.

When the Committee of Detail had structured the composition and it was duly examined and considered and amended, a Committee of Style was formed. That is my favorite committee. It comprised William Samuel Johnson of Connecticut, Alexander Hamilton of New York, Madison of Virginia, Rufus King of Massachusetts, and Gouverneur Morris of Pennsylvania. Apparently

Morris did the actual writing. And it is this document, produced by the Committee of Style and approved by the convention, that was called the Constitution of the United States. And for the first time in the various drafts there appeared in the preamble the phrase "We the people of the United States," thus quietly absorbing both the seminal idea of the Declaration of Independence and the continental vision of federalism.

THE VOICE OF THE CONSTITUTION

So we come back to this question of text. It is true but not sufficient to say that the Constitution reads as it does because it was written by a committee of lawyers. Something more is going on here. Every written composition has a voice, a persona, a character of presentation, whether by design of the author or not. The voice of the Constitution is a quiet voice. It does not rally us; it does not call on self-evident truths; it does not arm itself with philosophy or political principle; it does not argue, explain, condemn, excuse, or justify. It is postrevolutionary. Not claiming righteousness, it is, however, suffused with rectitude. It is this way because it seeks standing in the world, the elevation of the unlawful acts of men—unlawful first because the British government has been overthrown, and second because the confederation of the states has been subverted—to the lawful standing of nationhood. All the *herein*'s and *whereas*'s and *thereof*'s are not only legalisms; they also happen to be the diction of the British Empire, the language of the deposed. Nothing has changed that much, the Constitution says, lying; we are nothing that you won't recognize.

But there is something more. The key verb of the text is *shall*, as in "All legislative powers herein granted shall be vested in a Congress of the United States which shall consist of a Senate and a House of Representatives," or "New States may be admitted by the Congress into this Union; but no new State shall be formed or erected within the jurisdiction of any other State." The Constitution does not explicitly concern itself with the grievances that brought it about. It is syntactically futuristic: it prescribes what is to come. It prophesies. Even today, living two hundred years into the prophecy, we read it and find it still ahead of us, still extending itself in time. The Constitution gives law and assumes for itself the power endlessly to give law. It ordains. In its articles and sections, one after another, it offers a ladder to heaven. It is cold, distant, remote as a voice from on high, self-authenticating.

Through most of history kings and their servitor churches did the ordaining, and always in the name of God. But here the people do it: "We the People . . . do ordain and establish this Constitution for the United States." And the word for God appears nowhere in the text. Heaven forbid! In fact, its very last stricture is that "no religious test shall ever be required as a qualification to any office or public trust under the United States."

The voice of the Constitution is the inescapably solemn self-consciousness of the people giving the law unto themselves. But since in the Judeo-Christian world of Western civilization all given law imitates God—God being the ultimate lawgiver—in affecting the transhuman voice of law, that dry monotone that disdains persuasion, the Constitution not only takes on the respectable sound of British statute, it more radically assumes the character of scripture.

The ordaining voice of the Constitution is scriptural, but in resolutely keeping the authority for its dominion in the public consent, it presents itself as the sacred text of secular humanism.

I wish Mrs. Brundage had told me that back in Wade Junior High School.

I wish Jerry Falwell's and Jimmy Swaggart's and Pat Robertson's teachers had taught them that back in their junior high schools.

THE SACRED TEXT

Now, it is characteristic of any sacred text that it has beyond its literal instruction tremendous symbolic meaning for the people who live by it. Think of the Torah, the Koran, the Gospels. The sacred text dispenses not just social order but spiritual identity.

And as the states each in its turn ratified the Constitution, usually not without vehement debate and wrangling, the public turned out in the streets of major cities for processions, festivities, with a fresh new sense of themselves and their future.

Every major city had its ship of state rolling through the streets, pulled by teams of horses—a carpentered ship on wheels rolling around the corners and down the avenues in full sail, and perhaps with a crew of boys in sailor uniforms. It was called, inevitably, *The Constitution* or *Federalism* or *Union*. Companies of militia would precede it, the music of fifes and drums surround it, and children run after it, laughing at the surreal delight.

Of all the ratification processions, Philadelphia's was the grandest. There was not only a ship of state, the *Union*, but a float in the shape of a great eagle, drawn by six horses bearing a representation of the Constitution framed and fixed on a staff, crowned with the cap of Liberty, the words THE PEOPLE in gold letters on the staff. Even more elaborate was a slow-rolling majestic float called the *New Roof*, the Constitution being seen, in this case, as a structure under which society took secure shelter. The New Roof of the Constitution stood on a carriage drawn by ten white horses. Ornamented with stars, the dome was supported by thirteen pillars, each representing a state; at the top of the dome was a handsome cupola surmounted by a figure of Plenty, bearing her cornucopia. If you like the quaint charm of that, I remind you that today we speak of the "framers" of the Constitution, not the "writers," which would be more exact and realistic and less mythologically adequate.

Behind the *New Roof* came 450 architects, house carpenters, saw makers and file cutters, just to let people know there was now a roof-building industry available for everyone.

A thirty-foot-long float displayed a carding machine, a spinning machine of eighty spindles, a lace loom, and a textile printer. There were military units in this procession, companies of light infantry and cavalry, and there were clergymen of every denomination.

There were city officials and schools in their entire enrollments, but more prominent were the members of various trades, each dressed in its working clothes and carrying some display or pulling some float in advertisement of itself—sailmakers and ship chandlers, cordwainers, coach builders, sign painters, clock- and watchmakers, fringe and ribbon weavers, bricklayers, tailors, spinning-wheel makers, carvers and gilders, coopers, blacksmiths, potters, wheelwrights, tinplate workers, hatters, skinners, breeches makers, gunsmiths, saddlers, stonecutters, bakers, brewers, barber-surgeons, butchers, tanners, curriers, and, I am pleased to say, printers, booksellers, and stationers.

So heavily weighted was the great Philadelphia procession with those tradesmen and artisans, it could just as easily have been a Labor Day parade. The newly self-determined America was showing its strength and pride as a republic of hard work, in contrast to the European domains of privilege and title and their attendant poverty system. The Constitution was America de-Europeanizing itself. A kind of fission was taking place, and now here was a working-class republic, carried on the backs first of its citizen-soldiers dressed in rough brown and sober black, and then on the shoulders of its artisans and skilled workers. That anyway was the symbolic idea, the mythology that almost immediately attached itself to the ratified Constitution. From the very beginning it took on a symbolic character that its writers, worried always that they might never get it ratified, could not have foreseen. We speak of the "miracle at Philadelphia." That same impulse was working then: the celebration of the sacred text, miracles being beyond mere human understanding, a cause for wonder and gratitude—in a word, supernatural.

THE SUBTEXT

Yet it is true also of sacred texts that when they create a spiritual community, they at the same time create a larger community of the excluded. The Philistines are excluded, or the pagans, or the unwashed.

Even as the Constitution was establishing its sacred self in the general mind, it was still the work, the composition, of writers; and the writers were largely patricians, not working men, much less women. They tended to be well educated, wealthy, and not without self-interest. The historian Carl Degler says in *Out of Our Past:* "No new social class came to power through the doors of the American Revolution. The men who engineered the revolt were largely members of the colonial ruling class." That holds for the Philadelphia fifty-five. They themselves were aware of the benefits, if not to themselves, then to their class, of the provision guaranteeing the debts incurred under the Confederation: the security holders, the creditors of America, stood to make a lot of money; at the same time, the debtors—the freeholders, the small farmers—stood to lose everything. It was a practical document in their minds. They did not think of themselves as Founding Fathers or framers or anything more august than a group of men who held natural stewardship of the public welfare by virtue of their experience and background. They were concerned to establish a free and independent nation, but also a national economic order that would allow them to conduct business peaceably, profitably, and in the stable circumstances deriving from a strong central government.

The ideals of political democracy do not always accord with the successful conduct of business. Thus, as conceived in 1787, only the House of Representatives would be elected by popular vote. Senators were to be elected by state legislatures, and the president by an electoral college, meaning men like themselves who would command the votes of their localities. There was the sense in these strictures of a need for checks and balances against popular majorities. Furthermore, to come up with a piece of paper that diverse regional business interests could agree on meant cutting deals. One such deal was between the Northeastern states and the Southern. Importation of slaves would be allowed for twenty more years; in return only a simple majority in Congress would be required to pass navigational commerce acts that the seagoing Atlantic states much wanted. That odious deal appears, in part, in Article IV of the original Constitution. The exactness and precision of statute language in this case is used not to clarify but to euphemize a practice recognizably abhorrent to the writers:

> No person held to service or labour in one State under the laws thereof, escaping into another, shall, in consequence of any law or regulation therein, be discharged from such service or labour, but shall be delivered up on claim of the party to whom such service or labour may be due.

There is no mention of the word *slave*, yet a slave in one state became a slave in all. The Virginia delegate, George Mason, to my mind the great if inadvertent hero of the convention, warned his colleagues: "As nations cannot be rewarded or punished in the next world they must in this. By an inevitable chain of causes and effects, Providence punishes national sins by national calamities." If you affect the scriptural voice, he could have been telling them, you had better aspire to enlightenment, or the power of prophecy of your speech will work against you. And so it came to pass. That odious article worked through a historic chain of cause and effect like a powder fuse, until the country blew apart seventy-five years later in civil war. Not until 1865, with the passage of the Thirteenth Amendment, was slavery outlawed in the United States. And the monumental cost in lives, black and white, of that war, and the cost to the black people, the tragedy of their life in the antebellum South, and to American blacks everywhere since then (the state poll taxes that kept black people from voting in the South were not outlawed until the Twenty-fourth Amendment was ratified, in 1964), show how potent, how malignly powerful, the futuristic, transhuman Constitution has been where it has been poorly written. What was sacred is profane; there is a kind of blasphemous inversion of the thing.

In this formulation it is the power of the Constitution to amend itself, or, in writers' terms, to accept revision, that shows the delegates at their best. They knew what they had was imperfect, a beginning; Franklin and Washington said as much. Nevertheless, Mason refused to put his name to the constitutional document even after Franklin urged a unanimous presentation to the states, because of the slavery article and also because there was no Bill of Rights—no explicit statutes on the rights of American citizens to free speech and assembly and religious practice, and to speedy trial by jury of defendants in criminal charges; no prohibition against government search and seizure without judicial warrant; no guarantee of a free press and so forth. Alexander Hamilton argued that those things were implicit in the Constitution and did not have to be spelled out, much as people now say the Equal Rights Amendment is unnecessary, but Mason, to his credit, knew that they must be spelled out, which is to say written. Imagine where we would be today if Mason had not held his ground and if the lack of a Bill of Rights had not been taken up as the major concern of the antifederalists, such as Patrick Henry. We would today be trusting our rights and liberties to the reading of Attorney General Edwin Meese, who believes that people who are defendants in criminal trials are probably guilty or they would not be defendants, and who has said that the American Civil Liberties Union is essentially a criminals' lobby. George Mason's amendments, the first ten, were passed on to the states for ratification by the first elected Congress in 1791.

It is true of most of the sacred texts, I think, that a body of additional law usually works itself up around the primary material, and also achieves the force of prophecy. The Torah has its Talmud, and the Koran its *hadith,* and the New Testament its apostolic teachings. In like manner we have our sacred secular humanist amendments. Mythic or sacred time is endless, of course, and it was not until 1920, with the passage of the Nineteenth Amendment, that the women of the United States achieved suffrage. (I am told that this amendment has still not been ratified by the state of Georgia.)

HERMENEUTICS

Notice at this point a certain change of tone: my song of the miracle of Philadelphia has wobbled a bit; my voice has broken, and here I am speaking in the bitter caw of the critic. Yet there is a kind of inevitability to this. One cannot consider the Constitution of the United States without getting into an argument with it. It is the demand of the sacred text that its adherents not just believe in it but engage to understand its meanings, its values, its revelation. One finds every day in the newspapers the continuing argument with the Constitution, as different elements of society represent their versions of its truth. President Reagan argues with it, Attorney General Meese argues with it, and so, as a defenseless citizen, from a different point of view, do I. And, of course, the federal judiciary has amended, interpreted, and derived law from it. From the days of the great John Marshall on down—way down—to the days of William Rehnquist, the courts have not just worshiped the Constitution; they have read it. Their readings are equivalent to the priestly commentaries that accrue to every sacred text, and the commentaries on the commentaries, and we have two hundred years of these as statute and opinion.

It is the nature of the sacred text, speaking from the past to the present and into the future in that scriptural voice that does not explain, embellish itself, provide the source of its ideas or the intentions from which it is written, but which is packed with wild history—the self-authenticating text that is pared of all emotions in the interest of clear and precise law-giving—it is the nature of such a text, paradoxically, to shimmer with ambiguity and to become finally enigmatic, as if it were the ultimate voice of Buddhist self-realization.

And so I find here in my reflections a recapitulation of the debate of American constitutional studies of the past two hundred years, in the same manner that ontogeny is supposed to recapitulate phylogeny. Thus it was in the nineteenth century that historians such as George Bancroft celebrated the revolutionary nature of the Founding Fathers' work, praising them for having conceived of a republic of equal rights under law, constructed from the materials of the European Enlightenment but according to their own pragmatic Yankee design—a federalism of checks and balances that would withstand the worst buffetings of history, namely the Civil War, in the aftermath of which Bancroft happened to be writing.

Then in the early part of the twentieth century, when the worst excesses of American business were coming to light, one historian, Charles Beard, looked at old Treasury records and other documents and discovered enough to assert that the Fathers stood to gain personally from the way they put the thing together, at least their class did; that they were mostly wealthy men and lawyers; and that the celebrated system of checks and balances, rather than ensuring a distribution of power and a democratic form of government, in fact could be seen as having been devised to control populist sentiment and prevent a true majoritarian politics from operating in American life at the expense of property rights. Madison had said as much, Beard claimed, in *Federalist* number 10, which he wrote to urge ratification. Beard's economic interpretation of the Constitution has ever since governed scholarly debate. At the end of the Depression a neo-Beardian, Merrill Jensen, looked again at the post-Revolutionary period and came up with a thesis defending the Articles of Confederation as the true legal instrument of the Revolution, which, with modest amendments, could have effected the peace and order of the states with more democracy than a centralist government. In fact, he argued, there was no crisis under the Articles or danger of anarchy, except in the minds of the wealthy men who met in Philadelphia.

But countervailing studies appeared in the 1950s, the era of postwar conservatism, that showed Beard's research to be inadequate, asserting, for instance, that there were as many wealthy men of the framers' class who were against ratification as who were for it, or that men of power and influence tended to react according to the specific needs of their own states and localities, coastal or rural, rather than according to class.

And in the 1960s, the Kennedy years, a new argument appeared describing the Constitutional Convention above all as an exercise of democratic politics, a nationalist reform caucus that was genuinely patriotic, improvisational, and always aware that what it did must win popular approval if it was to become the law of the land.

In my citizen's self-instruction I embrace all of those interpretations. I believe all of them. I agree that something unprecedented and noble was created in Philadelphia; but that the economic self-interest of a bunch of businessmen was a large part of it; but that it was democratic and improvisational; but that it was, at the same time, something of a coup. I think all of those theories are true, simultaneously.

THE TWO-HUNDREDTH YEAR

And what of constitutional scholarship today, in the Age of Reagan?

Well, my emphasis on text, my use of textual analogy, responds to the work over the past few years of a new generation of legal scholars who have been arguing among themselves whether the Constitution can be seen usefully as a kind of literary text, sustaining intense interpretive reading—as a great poem, say—or better perhaps as a form of scripture. I have swiveled to embrace both of those critiques too, but adding, as a professional writer, that when I see the other professions become as obsessively attentive to text as mine is, I suspect it is a sign that we live in an age in which the meanings of words are dissolving, in which the culture of discourse itself seems threatened. That is my view of America under Reagan today: in literary critical terms, I would describe his administration as deconstructionist.

And so, by way of preservation, text consciousness may have arisen among us, law professors no less than novelists, as in medieval times monks began painstakingly copying the crumbling parchments to preserve them.

All told, it is as if the enigmatic constitutional text cannot be seen through, but, shimmering in ambiguity, dazzles back at each generation in its own times and struggles. It is as if the ambiguity is not in the text but in us, as we struggle in our natures—our consciences with our appetites, our sense of justice with our animal fears and self-interests—just as the Founding Fathers struggled so with their Constitution, providing us with a mirror of ourselves to go on shining, shining back at us through the ages, as the circumstances of our lives change, our costumes change, our general store is transformed into a mile-long twenty-four-hour shopping mall, our trundle carts transmogrify into rockets in space, our country paves over, and our young republic becomes a plated armory of ideological warfare: a mirror for us to see who we are and who we would like to be, the sponsors of private armies of thugs and rapists and murderers, or the last best hope of mankind.

It may be that as a result of World War II and the past forty years of our history we are on the verge, as a nation, of some characterological change that neither the federalists of the convention nor the antifederalists who opposed them could have foreseen or endorsed. We are evolving under realpolitik circumstances into a national military state—with a militarized economy larger than, and growing at the expense of, a consumer economy; a militarized scientific-intellectual establishment; and a bureaucracy of secret paramilitary intelligence agencies—that becomes increasingly self-governing and unlegislated. There may be no news in any of this. What may be news, however, is the extent to which the present administration* has articulated a rationale for this state of being, so that the culture too, both secular and religious, can be seen as beginning to conform to the needs of a national security state. More than any previous administration, this one apotheosizes not law but a carelessness or even contempt of law, as internationally it

---

* President Reagan's.

scorns the World Court and domestically it refuses to enforce federal civil rights statutes or honor the decrees of judicial review, or
gives into private hands the conduct of foreign policy outlawed by
the Congress. And more than any previous administration this one
discourses not in reason and argument but in demagogic pieties. Its
lack of reverence for law and contempt for language seem to go
hand in hand.

By contrast, I call your attention to the great genius of the convention of 1787, which was its community of discourse. The law it
designed found character from the means of its designing. Something arose from its deliberations, however contentious, and that
was the empowering act of composition given to people who know
what words mean and how they must be valued. Nobody told
anybody else to love it or leave it; nobody told anybody else to go
back where they came from; nobody suggested disagreement was
disloyalty; and nobody pulled a gun. Ideas, difficult ideas, were
articulated with language and disputed with language and took
their final fate, to be passed or rejected, as language. The possibility
of man-made law with the authority, the moral imperative, of
God's law, inhered in the process of making it.

That is what we celebrate as citizens today. That is what we
cherish and honor, a document that gives us the means by which
we may fearlessly argue ourselves into clarity as a free and unified
people. To me the miracle at Philadelphia was finally the idea of
democratic polity, a foot in the door of the new house for all mankind. The relentless logic of a Constitution in the name of the people is that a national state exists for their sake, not the other way
around. The undeviating logic of a Constitution in the name of the
people is that the privilege of life under its domain is equitable,
which is to say, universal. That you cannot have democracy only
for yourself or your club or your class or your church or your clan
or your color or your sex, for then the word doesn't mean what it
says. That once you write the prophetic text for a true democracy—
as our forefathers did in their draft and as our amending legislators
and judiciary have continued to do in their editing of its moral self-

contradictions and methodological inadequacies—that once this text is in voice, it cannot be said to be realized on earth until all the relations among the American people, legal relations, property relations, are made just.

And I reflect now, in conclusion, that this is what brought the people into the streets in Philadelphia two hundred years ago, those wheelwrights and coach builders and ribbon and fringe weavers: the idea, the belief, the faith, that America was unprecedented.

I'd like to think, in this year of bicentennial celebration, that the prevailing image will be of those plain people taking to the streets, those people with only their wit and their skills to lead them through their lives, forming their processions: the wheelwrights and ribbon makers, the railroad porters and coal miners, the garment workers, the steelworkers, the automobile workers, the telephone operators, the air traffic controllers, the farm workers, the computer programmers, and, one hopes, the printers, stationers, and booksellers too.

A Citizen's Reading

A good annotated constitutional text at the secondary-school level is *Your Rugged Constitution*, by Bruce and Esther Findlay (Stanford University Press, 1952). Of the available dramatic reconstructions of the Constitutional Convention of 1787, I relied most heavily on *The Great Rehearsal*, by Carl Van Doren (Viking, 1948). All popular studies of the convention depend on the original scholarship of Max Farrand, whose *The Framing of the Constitution of the United States* (Yale University Press, 1913) is a classic contribution.

My view of the sociopolitical ferment in America before and after the Revolution owes much to Howard Zinn's *A People's History of the United States* (Harper & Row, 1980), a bracing antidote to complacent historiography, and to *The Americans*, by J. C. Furnas (G. P. Putnam's Sons, 1969), a compendious examination of daily life from the colonial period to the twentieth century. My summary of the scholarly debate from Bancroft and Beard on through the 1960s would have been difficult without *Essays on the Making of the Constitution*, edited by Leonard W. Levy (Oxford University Press, 1969). This astute anthology presents the central ideas of the major constitutional historians in excerpt, thus relieving the lay person of the necessity of reading their important works in entirety.

Finally, although the following scholars may take exception to the uses I've made of their work, I credit my conversion to constitutional scripturalism to James Boyd White, "The Judicial Opinion and the Poem: Ways of Reading, Ways of Life" (*Michigan Law Review*, Vol. 82:1669, 1984), and "Law as Language: Reading Law and Reading Literature" (*Texas Law Review*, Vol. 60:415, 1982); Thomas C. Grey, "The Constitution as Scripture" (*Stanford Law Review*, Vol. 37:1, 1984); and Sanford Levinson, "The Constitution in American Civil Religion" (*Supreme Court Review*, 1979).—E.L.D.

(1987)

The Nineteenth
New York

We make a mistake to condescend to the past as if it were preparatory to our own time. New York in the nineteenth century was more creative, more deadly, more of a genius society, than it is now. It was high tech, heavily into railroading and telegraphy. Rotary presses put tens of thousands of newspapers on the streets for a penny or two. Enormous steam engines powered the mills and manufactories. Gas lamps lit the city at night. Public schools flourished. A city board of health enacted sanitation reforms that ended epidemic cholera.

The war of secession made New York rich. When it was over there was nothing to stop progress—no classical ruins of ideas, no superstitions, to retard civil republican ardor. Not that much had to be destroyed or overturned, as in the European cultures of Roman towns and medieval guilds. A few Dutch farms were razed, villages melded into towns, towns burned into precincts, and all at once block and tackle were raising the marble and granite mansions of Fifth Avenue, and burly roundsmen were wading through the stopped traffic on Broadway, slapping horses on the rumps, disengaging carriage wheels, and cursing the heedless entanglement of horsecars, stages, drays, and two-in-hands by which the people undertook to drive themselves into their business day.

The air was bad then too. Cinderous locomotives ran down the avenues on elevated tracks. Coal stoked the steamships and the ferries. At night the flaming stacks of the foundries on the Jersey shore cast torchlight like seed over the old wharves and packing sheds of the West Side. Cookstoves in homes burned coal, and on a winter morning without wind, black plumes rose from the chimneys in orderly rows, like the shimmering citizens of a necropolis.

Not church spires but fire towers were the tallest structures. Fire wardens tapped their telegraph keys and after a few minutes the hose companies came at a gallop.

The city's water-supply system was put in place in the 1840s. From a string of Catskill lakes, the water flowed through Westchester in conduits, crossed the Harlem River on the High Bridge viaduct of fifteen Roman arches, and came to rest lapping the cobblestoned banks of the Croton Distributing Reservoir at Forty-second Street and Fifth Avenue, where the New York Public Library stands today.

Of course, in the antebellum era, Forty-second and Fifth was the northern edge of civilization. Central Park, well to the north, was not yet unfolded, a wreckage of nature, all mudholes and ditches and berms of shoveled earth, a park still in the minds of its imaginers. So everyone went to the reservoir. The retaining walls were twenty-five feet thick and rose forty-four feet high in a kind of Egyptian slant. The corners were relieved by trapezoidal turrets, and bisecting each long wall face were temple doors. You went in, climbed up a stair and came out in the sky. It was at the reservoir people soothed their spirits, walking arm in arm with their friends along the parapet. If they wanted a breeze in summer, here is where it would blow. Puffs rippled the water. Children launched their toy sloops. From this elevation the rising city seemed to fall back before something that wasn't a city, a squared expanse of black water that was in fact the geometric absence of a city. This was the closest they could come to pastoral.

The Egyptian motif held too in "the Tombs," the municipal prison on Centre Street, a block-square, two-story columned structure with sun-god embellishments. But the nineteenth-century city copied nearly every style of the past—classical Greek, Romanesque, Second Empire, Belle Epoque, Gothic, and Moorish. New York in the nineteenth was a bizarre, endlessly self-revising culture of ancestor worship. Its most original architectural idea was to house the immigrant millions in Tenement.

Our generations were raw, spiritually unformed. Our literature was just proposing itself, and our national character was so cloven, so self-contentious, as to be undetermined. The people were given to rioting. They rioted when flour went from seven to twenty dollars a barrel, when abolitionists spoke; they burned the Colored Orphan Asylum on Fifth Avenue when Lincoln ordered conscription. There were gang riots when the Dead Rabbits clashed with the Roach Guards, and police riots when the old-guard Municipals fought the usurper Metropolitans.

Armies of newsboys battled for their corners, Hibernian societies attacked Orangemen's parades, churchmen thundered from their pulpits, thieves in soft caps sapped thieves in tall hats, and matrons pointedly did not invite one another to their balls. Ragpickers, a professional class, roamed the streets.

After the war the Tweed Ring created a model for systematic corruption that is the envy of politicians to this day. The Wall Street stock frauds, insider-trading schemes, and market-cornering conspiracies of the time have never in our century been surpassed, though not for lack of trying. The theme of the nineteenth was excess, excess in everything—pleasure, gaudy display, endless toil, and death. Vagrant children slept in the alleys. A conspicuously self-satisfied class of new wealth and weak intellect was all aglitter in a setting of mass misery. Walt Whitman renders some of his feeling for the time in his poem "Song of Myself." He was the city's bard, among other things, and not all that unknown.

> *Somehow I have been stunned. Stand back!*
> *Give me a little time beyond my cuffed head and slumbers*
> *and dreams and gaping . . .*

I deliberately leave out of this reverie the colossal figures, the politicians, newspapermen, artists and writers, clerics, criminals, merchants and millionaires by which we identify the postwar decades of the nineteenth New York. Somehow, individual personality confuses the matter. It is easier to feel their culture in the aggregate. We move among the silent decisions of the nineteenth-century dead. It is their spirit that directs us—in their street names and configurations, in the technology they devised, in their buildings still standing, and, hauntingly, in the structures long razed. They made New York a global city, the place to come to from every part of the world, the place to be. They invested a lot of money in a very small space. With their oyster bars, theaters, saloons, racecourses, beer gardens, dance halls, and brothels, they proposed an ethic of human insatiability. From them we inherit, in any moment's crowding at the intersection of two New York City streets, a vision of the anarchy of human intent. And New York, as the point of convergence of many of the world's cultures, suggests the unreality of all of them.

The islanded city grew not up but in a northerly direction, and its citizens were taught twentieth-century time by the speed with which acreage was covered in paving stones. One day a limestone mansion would appear in a field. The next day it stood on a city street with horse and carriage riding by. The frontier was pioneered often by charities. The nineteenth tended to put its welfare institutions as far out of town as possible, behind stone walls and high hedges. Orphanages, insane asylums, poorhouses, sanatoriums, and mission homes for fallen women were built far uptown—in Washington Heights or on the North River, where the land was cheap, or on the East River islands.

Today, from Franklin D. Roosevelt Drive you can see the ruins of the old city almshouse standing on the south end of Blackwell's Island. The astonishing thing in this city celebrated for tearing itself down and beginning again every generation or so is how much of the nineteenth is still visible. The Federal-style brick town houses in the West Village . . . the Jefferson Market Library . . . the great voluminous brownstone Cooper Union college on Astor Place, where Lincoln spoke . . . the stolid rows on West Twenty-third Street where the well-to-do moved to get away from the noise of downtown . . . the Brooklyn Bridge . . . the Memorial arch at Washington Square . . . the esplanade in Central Park . . . the Armory on Park Avenue. . . . In every neighborhood, from the Lower East Side to Harlem, well kept or neglected, the century is still with us, the ghostly nineteenth.

On nights of fog you see it best. Look south, over lower Manhattan: A heavy fog works its way down through the architectural strata. First the World Trade Center disappears, then the fifty- and sixty-story office buildings of glass, then the early-twentieth-century stone Woolworth Building . . . story by story the skyline blacks out, modernity deconstructs, and all that is left is the nineteenth-century city. Its grandeur is ground level. You can walk down Greene Street, in the fine mist, past the iron fronts, and know that this is the city that Melville saw.

The nineteenth is quietly with us in all sorts of fogs and dreams. Perhaps it is, after all, a ghost city that stands to contemporary New York as some panoramic negative print. It is reversed in its lights and shadows, and its seasons are turned around. It is a companion city of the other side, some moral hologram generated from an unknown but intense radiation of historical energy and randomly come to imprint on our dreaming brains.

So I won't here write of New York's actual history, the famous murders, fires, riots, strikes, conventions, state visits, and other momentous events that, if they were marked, would stipple the city in brass plaques. Let one parade stand for all: the slow march that was like a commencement procession for our century—the funereal march carrying the body of Abraham Lincoln up Broadway. For, of course, centuries don't neatly end and begin centennially, but in their middles, in their accidental years of spiritual prophecy.

We can look at the steel engravings that were made on that day and think of the city as silent, as if etched into history on an engraver's pen. But a hushed crowd is not silent: There was a restless sibilance, a rustling, an intoned exhalation of grief; people pushed and shoved, shoulder to shoulder, and cried and muttered opinions to the air. Some took it upon themselves to narrate what they saw to others seeing the same thing, as if it weren't enough to look, as if the sight brought forth words as a church service brought forth prayer or psalm. They spoke of the caisson as it was coming, and described it as it went by, and suggested what it had looked like when it had passed. Children were held aloft and instructed to commit the scene to memory: an immense military procession, seemingly endless blocks of funereal infantry followed by a company of cavalry, the horses dressed with head plumes, and then, in a hollow moving square of men, the ornate hearse itself, canopied and bunted and draped in the color that buries color, the color that eclipses light and life. A puzzling parade to a young eye, perhaps even disappointing, lacking cannon, lacking the martial spirit, and a drummed-out military music to set the pace.

The Union's flags flew from the rooftops at half-mast and from the hearse in gathers dipped in deference to death. . . . The hoisted frowning child watched the hearse, which seemed reluctant to bear its burden, and heard the muffled drums and the independently rhythmed footfall of horses alone with their task, the incredibly ordinary stamp of horse's foot upon the pavement being now a monumental sound in the unnaturally chastened city.

And set alone in the middle of all this rustling pushing watching, the subject of everyone's attention, was the thing that could not be seen, a body in its box, recumbent and hidden like any body given for burial, recumbent and hidden with its hands across its breast, while his famous face glowed in the child's brain, the long, homely, sad-eyed face so immense in death as to be construed by public grief in the cloud formations hovering over the sunless city, and evoking, as the pathetic coffin could not, the moral immensity of what had happened.

Some regnant purpose was enshrouded in his death, but what was it? He had not been reasonable to suggest by his martyrdom a noble plane of thought beyond the reach of most of us.

But for weeks afterward, remnants and tatters of the funereal muslin, torn by wind and rain, hung from the windows of the parade route. Black dye stains marred the façades of the limestone buildings and blotted the awnings of the shops and restaurants. The city was unnaturally still. People were not themselves. The Union veterans, with their pinned-up sleeves and crutches at the entrance of A. T. Stewart's department store, saw coins rain into their tin cups.

And then some soulless, social resolve began to work itself out of his grave and rise again. And the city's new century began.

(1992)

FALSE DOCUMENTS

Fiction is a not entirely rational means of discourse. It gives to the reader something more than information. Complex understandings, indirect, intuitive, and nonverbal, arise from the words of the story, and by a ritual transaction between reader and writer, instructive emotion is generated in the reader from the illusion of suffering an experience not his own. A novel is a printed circuit through which flows the force of a reader's own life.

Sartre in his essay "Literature and Existentialism" says: ". . . each book is a recovery of the totality of being . . . For this is quite the final goal of art: to recover this world by giving it to be seen as it is, but as if it had its source in human freedom."

Certainly I know that I would rather read a sentence such as this from Nabokov's *The Gift*—

As he crossed toward the pharmacy at the corner he involuntarily turned his head because of a burst of light that had ricocheted from his temple, and saw, with that quick smile with which we greet a rainbow or a rose, a blindingly white parallelogram of sky being unloaded from the van—a dresser with mirror, across which, as across a cinema screen, passed a flawlessly clear reflection of boughs, sliding and swaying not arboreally, but with a human vacillation, produced by the nature of those who were carrying this sky, these boughs, this gliding facade.

—whose occasion is in question, whose truth I cannot test, than a sentence such as this from the rational mentality of *The New York Times*—

> The Navy has announced base consolidations and other actions that it said would eliminate 500 civilian jobs and 16 military positions at an annual savings of about five million dollars.

—whose purposes are immediately clear, and with regard to whose truth I am completely credulous.

As a writer of fiction I could make the claim that a sentence spun from the imagination, i.e., a sentence composed as a lie, confers upon the writer a degree of perception or acuity or heightened awareness—some additional usefulness—that a sentence composed with the most strict reverence for fact does not. In any event, what can surely be distinguished here is two kinds of power in language, the power of the Navy's announcement residing in its manifest reference to the verifiable world—let us call that *the power of the regime*—and the power of Nabokov's description inhering in a private or ideal world that cannot be easily corroborated or verified— let us call that *the power of freedom.*

Immediately I have to wonder if this formulation is too grandiose —the power of the regime and the power of freedom. But it is true that we live in an industrial society which counts its achievements from the discoveries of science and which runs on empirical thinking and precise calculations. In such a society language is conceived primarily as the means by which facts are communicated. Language is seen as a property of facts themselves—their persuasive property. We are taught that facts are to be distinguished from feeling and that feeling is what we are permitted for our rest and relaxation when the facts get us down. This is the bias of scientific method and empiricism by which the world reveals itself and gives itself over to our control insofar as we recognize the primacy of fact-reality. We all kick the rock to refute Berkeley.

So what I suppose I mean by *the power of the regime* is first of all the modern consensus of sensibility that could be called *realism,* which, since there is more than epistemology to this question of knowing the world, may be defined as the business of getting on and producing for ourselves what we construe as the satisfaction of our needs—and doing it with standards of measure, market studies, contracts, tests, polls, training manuals, office memos, press releases, and headlines.

But I shall go further: If we are able to recognize and name any broad consensus of sensibility we are acknowledging its rule. Anything which governs us must by necessity be self-interested and organized to continue itself. Therefore I have to conclude that the regime of facts is not from God but man-made, and, as such, infinitely violable. For instance, it used to be proposed as a biological fact that women were emotionally less stable and intellectually less capable than men. What we proclaim as the discovered factual world can be challenged as the questionable world we ourselves have painted—the cultural museum of our values, dogmas, assumptions, that prescribes for us not only what we may like and dislike, believe and disbelieve, but also what we may be permitted to see and not to see.

And so I am led to affirm my phraseology. There is a regime language that derives its strength from what we are supposed to be and a language of freedom whose power consists in what we threaten to become. And I'm justified in giving a political character to the nonfictive and fictive uses of language because there is conflict between them.

It is possible there was a time in which the designative and evocative functions of language were one and the same. I remember being taught that in school. The sun was Apollo's chariot in fact as well as fiction—the chariot was metaphor and operative science at one and the same time. The gods have very particular names and powers and emotions in Homer. They go about deflecting arrows, bringing on human rages, turning hearts, and controlling history. Nevertheless there really was a Troy and a Trojan war. Alone among the arts, literature confuses fact and fiction. In the Bible the natural and supernatural flow into each other, man and God go hand in hand. Even so, there are visible to our own time volcanoes that are pillars of fire by night and pillars of cloud by day.

I conclude there must have been a world once in which the act of telling a story was in itself a presumption of truth. It was not necessarily a better world than our own, but as a writer of fiction I can see the advantages to my craft of not having a reader question me and ask if what I've written is true—that is, if it really happened. In our society there is no presumption of truth in the art of storytelling except in the minds of children. We have complex understandings of the different functions of language and we can all recognize the aesthetic occasion and differentiate it from a "real" one. This means to me that literature is less a tool for survival than it once was. In ancient times, presumably, the storyteller got a spot near the fire because the story he told defined the powers to which the listener was subject and suggested how to live with them. Literature was as valuable as a club or a sharpened bone. It bound the present to the past, the visible with the invisible, and it helped to compose the community necessary for the continuing life of its members.

In Walter Benjamin's brilliant essay "The Story Teller: Reflections on the Works of Nikolai Leskov," we're told that storytelling in the Middle Ages was primarily a means of giving counsel. The resident master craftsman and traveling journeyman worked together in the same room and stories passed between them in the rhythm of their work. Thus each story was honed by time and many tellers. If the story was good, the counsel was valuable and therefore the story was true. "The art of story telling is coming to an end," Benjamin says, writing in 1936. "Less and less frequently do we encounter people with the ability to tell a tale properly. . . . one reason for this is obvious: experience has fallen in value . . . we are not richer but poorer in communicable experience."

For our sins, Benjamin implies, we have the novelist, an isolated individual who gives birth to his novel whole, himself uncounseled and without the ability to counsel others. "In the midst of life's fullness, the novel gives evidence of the profound perplexity of the living," he says. "The first great novel, *Don Quixote*, teaches how the spiritual greatness, the boldness, the helpfulness, of one of the noblest of men, Don Quixote, are completely devoid of counsel and do not contain the slightest scintilla of wisdom."

—

But I am interested in the ways, not peculiar to itself, that *Don Quixote* does its teaching. And of special significance I think is Cervantes' odd claim that he cannot be considered the author of his book. In Part 1, Chapter 9, for instance, he introduces the Don's adventures that follow by claiming to have come across an account of them, on parchment, by an Arab historian, in a marketplace in Toledo. "I bought all the parchments for half a real," he confides. "But if the merchant had had any sense and had known how much I wanted them he might have demanded and got more than six reales from the sale."

I look at another great early fiction, *Robinson Crusoe*, and see that it is treated by its author in much the same way. There is a Robinson Crusoe and this is his memoir, and Daniel Defoe has only edited this book for him. As editor, Defoe can assure us, with all the integrity naturally falling to his profession, that the story is true. "The editor believes the thing to be a just history of fact," he says. "Neither is there any appearance of fiction in it."

So both of these classic practitioners dissociate themselves from the work, apparently as a means of gaining authority for the narrative. They use other voices than their own in the composition and present themselves not as authors but as literary executors. In the excellent phrase of Kenneth Rexroth, they adopt the convention of the "false document."

I'm not familiar enough with their publishing histories to know the degree of gullibility with which these false documents were originally received by their readers. Certainly the parodic intentions of *Don Quixote* were explicit. But the romances of chivalry and pastoral love that punctuate the narrative stand in contrast to the realistic humiliations of the Don. Cervantes complains at the beginning of Part 2 of *Don Quixote* that other writers have, subsequent to the great success of Part 1, written their own histories of the same person. In fact, he has Quixote and Sancho Panza review their representations in the piratical works, thus conferring upon themselves an additional falsely documented reality. But let us grant Cervantes' audience, and Defoe's as well, a gullibility no greater than ironic appreciation: In order to have its effect, a false document need only be possibly true. The transparency of the pretense does not damage it. A man named Alexander Selkirk, who had been a castaway, was famous in Defoe's London, and all the English readers needed to know to read *Crusoe* and to believe it was that there were others who could have had Selkirk's experience. . . .

—

Of course every fiction is a false document in that compositions of words are not life. But I speak specifically of the novelist's act of creative disavowal by which the text he offers takes on some additional authority because he did not write it, or latterly, because he claims it was impossible to write it.

I come back for a moment to *Robinson Crusoe:* As a false document it interests me enormously. It was published at a time when the life adventures of Alexander Selkirk had been well broadcast in London for several years. In fact, Selkirk's autobiography had been published and there is reason to believe Defoe actually interviewed him. Selkirk was a clearly unstable, tormented individual. His months alone on an island had so wrecked what equanimity he had that when he was restored to London he immediately built himself a cave in his garden, and he lived in the cave and sulked and raged, an embarrassment to his family and a menace to his neighbors. Defoe turned this disturbed person into the stout, resolute Englishman (Crusoe), a genius at survival by the grace of his belief in God and in the white European race.

And inevitably, Crusoe the composition has obscured Selkirk the man, whose great gift to civilization, we see now, was in providing Daniel Defoe the idea for a story. The story tells what happens when an urban Englishman is removed from his environment and plunked down in nature. What happens is that he defines the national character.

But the point about this first of the great false documents in English is that at the moment of its publication there was an indwelling of the art in the real life; everyone in London who read *Crusoe* knew about Selkirk, there was intravention, a mixing-up of the historic and the aesthetic, the real and the possibly real. And what was recovered was the state of wisdom that existed, for Walter Benjamin, before fact and fiction became ontologically differentiated— that is, when it was possible for fiction to give counsel.

The novelist deals with his isolation by splitting himself in two, creator and documentarian, teller and listener, conspiring to pass on the collective wisdom in its own language, disguised in its own enlightened bias, that of the factual world.

———

It is not a bad system, but it gets the writer into trouble. To offer facts to the witness of the imagination and pretend they are real is to commit a kind of regressive heresy. The language of politicians, historians, journalists, and social scientists always presumes a world of fact discovered, and, like a religious tenet, the presumption is held more fiercely the more it is seen to be illusory.

Fiction writers are at best inconvenient, like some old relative in mismatching pants and jacket who knocks on our door during a dinner party to remind us from what we come. Society has several ways of dealing with this inconvenience. The writer is given most leeway in the Western democracies which are the most industrially advanced. In these countries, where empiricism works so well as to be virtually unassailable, the writer-nuisance is relegated to the shadow world of modern aesthetics or culture, a nonintegral anti-universe with reflections of power rather than power, with a kind of shamanistic potence at best, subject to the whims of gods and spirits, an imitation with words of the tangible real world of act and event and thunder.

In those countries which are not advanced industrial democracies the writer is treated with more respect. In Burma or Iran or Chile or Indonesia or the Soviet Union, it is understood that a writer using the common coin of the political speech or the press release or the newspaper editorial to compose facts in play has the power to do harm. He is recognized to have discovered the secret the politician is born knowing: that good and evil are construed, that there is no outrage, no monstrousness that cannot be made reasonable and logical and virtuous, and no shining act that cannot be turned to disgrace—with language.

Thus the American Center of PEN, the organization of novelists, poets, essayists, editors, and publishers, finds it necessary to distribute each year a poster entitled WRITERS IN PRISON. This poster, which is very large, simply lists the writers who are currently locked in cells or insane asylums or torture chambers in various countries around the world—who are by their being and profession threats to the security of political regimes. The imprisonment of writers is common in countries of the right and of the left, it doesn't seem to matter what the ideology. I know from the novelist Alexander Solzhenitsyn about the Gulag Archipelago, the network of Soviet prison camps and secret police in Siberia, but I know too from Reza Baraheni, the Iranian novelist and poet, about the Iranian secret police, SAVAK, and the torture of artists and intellectuals in Iranian prisons. Wherever citizens are seen routinely as enemies of their own government, writers are routinely seen to be the most dangerous enemies.

So that in most countries of the world literature is politics. All writers are by definition engagé. Even if they are timid gentle souls who write pastoral verses on remote farms, the searchlight will seek them out.

In this country we are embarrassed or angered by the excesses of repression of foreign petty tyrants and murderous bureaucracies. But apart from the excesses, the point of view is hardly unprecedented. Elizabethan writers lived in the shadow of the Tower and when Plato proposed his ideal republic he decreed that poets were to be outlawed. Part of our problem, as Americans, in failing to apprehend the relationship of art and politics is, of course, our national good fortune. . . . Our primary control of writers in the United States does not have to be violent—it operates on the assumption that aesthetics is a limited arena where, according to the rules, we may be shocked or threatened, but only in fun. The novelist need not be taken seriously because his work appeals largely to young people, women, intellectuals, and other pampered minorities, and, lacking any real currency, is not part of the relevant business of the nation.

—

If these thoughts were a story, the story would tell of a real tangible world and the writer's witness of that world in which some writers occasionally, by the grace of God, cause the real world to compose itself according to the witness, as our faces compose themselves in our mirrors.

However I detect a faint presumption of romance in my attitude, and I have to wonder why I suspect myself of being less than hospitable to the forms of nonfictive discourse, as if they were a team from another city. Nonfiction enjoys the sort of authority that has not easily been granted fiction since Walter Benjamin's storytellers traded their last tales. On the other hand it does give up something for the privilege; it is dulled by the obligation to be factual. This is acknowledged by the people who would not pick up a novel but who say of a particularly good biography or history that it reads like one.

Perhaps I feel that the nonfictive premise of a discoverable factual world is in itself a convention no less hoary than Cervantes' Arab historian.

Consider those occasions—criminal trials in courts of law—when society arranges with all its investigative apparatus to apprehend factual reality. Using the tested rules of evidence and the accrued wisdom of our system of laws, we determine the guilt or innocence of defendants and come to judgment. Yet the most important trials in our history, those which reverberate in our lives and have most meaning for our future, are those in which the judgment is called into question: Scopes, Sacco and Vanzetti, the Rosenbergs. Facts are buried, exhumed, deposed, contradicted, recanted. There is a decision by the jury and, when the historical and prejudicial context of the decision is examined, a subsequent judgment by history. And the trial shimmers forever with just that perplexing ambiguity characteristic of a true novel. . . .

"There are no facts in themselves," said Nietzsche. "For a fact to exist we must first introduce meaning." When a physicist invents an incredibly sophisticated instrument to investigate subatomic phenomena, he must wonder to what degree the instrument changes or creates the phenomena it reports. This problem was elucidated by Werner Heisenberg as the Principle of Uncertainty. At the highest level of scruple and reportorial disinterest there is the intrusive factor of an organized consciousness. At lower levels, in law, in political history, the intrusion is not instrumental but moral: Meaning must be introduced, and no judgment does not carry the passion of the judge.

We all know examples of history that doesn't exist. We used to laugh at the Russians, who in their encyclopedias attributed every major industrial invention to themselves. We knew how their great leaders who had fallen out of favor were erased from their history texts. We were innocent then: Our own school and university historians had done just the same thing to whole peoples who lived and died in this country but were seriously absent from our texts: Afro-American, Native American, Chinese. There is no history except as it is composed. There are no failed revolutions, only lawless conspiracies. All history is contemporary history, says Benedetto Croce in *History as the Story of Liberty*: "However remote in time events may seem to be, every historical judgment refers to present needs and situations." That is why history has to be written and rewritten from one generation to another. The act of composition can never end.

What is a historical fact? A spent shell? A bombed-out building? A pile of shoes? A victory parade? A long march? Once it has been suffered it maintains itself in the mind of witness or victim, and if it is to reach anyone else it is transmitted in words or on film and it becomes an image, which, with other images, constitutes a judgment. I am well aware that some facts, for example, the systematic murder by the Nazis and their client states of six million men, women, and children, are so indisputably monstrous as to seem to stand alone. But history shares with fiction a mode of mediating the world for the purpose of introducing meaning, and it is the cultural authority from which they both derive that illuminates those facts so that they can be perceived.

Facts are the images of history, just as images are the facts of fiction.

Of course it happens that the people most skeptical of history as a nonfictive discipline are the historians themselves. E. H. Carr, in his famous essay "The Historian and His Facts," speaks of history "as a continuous process of interaction" between the writer of history and his facts. Carr also quotes the American historian Carl Becker, who said: "The facts of history do not exist for any historian until he has created them." Neither man would be surprised by the tentative conclusions of the structuralist critic Roland Barthes, who, in an essay entitled "Historical Discourse," attempts to find the specific linguistic features that differentiate factual and imaginary narrative. "By structures alone," Barthes concludes, "historical discourse is essentially a product of ideology, or rather of imagination." In other words a visitor from another planet could not by study of the techniques of discourse distinguish composed fiction from composed history. The important stylistic device of composed history, the chaste or objective voice, one that gives no clues to the personality of the narrator, Barthes says, "turns out to be a particular form of fiction." (Teachers of English know that form as Realism.)

So that as a novelist considering this particular nonfictive discipline I could claim that history is a kind of fiction in which we live and hope to survive, and fiction is a kind of speculative history, perhaps a superhistory, by which the available data for the composition are seen to be greater and more various in their sources than the historian supposes.

—

At issue is the human mind, which has to be shocked, seduced, or otherwise provoked out of its habitual stupor. Even the biblical prophets knew they had to make it new. They shouted and pointed their fingers to heaven, but they were poets too, and dramatists. Isaiah walked abroad naked and Jeremiah wore a yoke around his neck to prophesy deportation and slavery, respectively, to their soon-to-be-deported-and-enslaved countrymen. Moral values are inescapably aesthetic. In the modern world it is the moral regime of factual reality that impinges on the provinces of art. News magazines present the events of the world as an ongoing weekly serial. Weather reports are constructed on television with exact attention to conflict (high pressure areas clashing with lows), suspense (the climax of tomorrow's weather prediction coming after the commercial), and other basic elements of narrative. The creating, advertising, packaging, and marketing of factual products is unquestionably a fictional enterprise. The novelist looking around him has inevitably to wonder why he is isolated by his profession when everywhere the factualists have appropriated his techniques and even brought a kind of exhaustion to the dramatic modes by the incessant exploitation of them.

Nevertheless, there is something we honor in the character of a journalist—whatever it is that makes him value reportorial objectivity and assure us at the same time that it is an unattainable ideal. We recognize and trust that combination of passion and humility. It is the religious temperament.

The virtues of the social sciences are even more appealing to us. Sociologists and social psychologists not only make communion with facts but in addition display the scientific method of dealing with them. The tale told by the social scientists, the counsel given, is nonspecific, collated, and subject to verification. Because they revise each other's work constantly and monitor themselves, as novelists do not, and are like a democracy in that the rule of this or that elevated theorist is subject to new elections every few years, we find them ingenuous and trustworthy. Today we read the empirical fictions of Konrad Lorenz or Oscar Lewis, B. F. Skinner or Eric Erikson, as we used to read Dickens and Balzac, for pleasure and instruction. The psychologists' and sociologists' compositions of facts seem less individualistic and thus more dependable than any random stubborn vision of which the novelist is capable. They propose to understand human character or to define it as a function of ethnic background, sexuality, age, economic class, and they produce composite portraits like those done in a police station—bad art, but we think we see someone we recognize. It is at least a possibility that the idea of human beings as demographic collections of traits, or as loci of cultural and racial and economic events, is exactly what is needed in our industrial society to keep the machines going. We have in such concepts as "complex," "sublimation," "repression," "identity crisis," "object relations," "borderline," and so on, the interchangeable parts of all of us. In this sense modern psychology is the industrialization of storytelling.

———

I am thus led to the proposition that there is no fiction or nonfiction as we commonly understand the distinction: There is only narrative.

But it is a novelist's proposition, I can see that very well. It is in my interest to claim that there is no difference between what I do and what everyone else does. I claim as I pull everyone else over to my side of the mirror that there is nothing between the given universe and our attempt to mediate it, there is no real power, only some hope that we might deny our own contingency.

And I am led to an even more pugnacious view—that the development of civilizations is essentially a progression of metaphors.

The novelist's opportunity to do his work today is increased by the power of the regime to which he finds himself in opposition. As clowns in the circus imitate the aerialists and tightrope walkers, first for laughs and then so that it can be seen that they do it better, we have it in us to compose false documents more valid, more real, more truthful than the "true" documents of the politicians or the journalists or the psychologists. Novelists know explicitly that the world in which we live is still to be formed and that reality is amenable to any construction that is placed upon it. It is a world made for liars and we are born liars. But we are to be trusted because ours is the only profession forced to admit that it lies—and that bestows upon us the mantle of honesty. "In a writer's eyes," said Emerson, "anything which can be thought can be written; the writer is the faculty of reporting and the universe is the possibility of being reported." By our independence of all institutions, from the family to the government, and with no responsibility to defend them from their own hypocrisy and murderousness, we are a valuable resource and an instrument of survival. There is no nonfictive discipline that does not rule out some element of the human psyche, that does not restrict some human energy and imprison it, that does not exclude some monstrous phantom of human existence. Unlike the politicians, we take office first and then create our constituencies, and that is to be a shade more arrogant than the politicians. But our justification and redemption is in emulating the false documents that we universally call our dreams. For dreams are the first false documents, of course: They are never real, they are never factual; nevertheless they control us, purge us, mediate our baser natures, and prophesy our fate.

(1977)

STANDARDS

G reat Songs and the Men Who Wrote Them. Invariably from poor families, possibly immigrants, coming to light only in their sixties or seventies (uncovered first by the archivists, inter-viewers, and professors of popular culture, then presented for eve-nings of song and reminiscence under the auspices of arts councils, then made the subjects of documentary films) because as compos-ers of classics they were thought to have died long ago. And so they rise like vampires from their coffins, toupees slightly askew. They have blondes on their arms who are taller than they, glittery silk-sheathed women highly made-up, past their prime, not as defini-tively the composers' juniors as they once were but still solemnly sexual. The first thing you notice about the men who wrote the songs is their rampant self-satisfaction. They talk to you nose to nose, grab your lapels, and inform you of everything you have to know about their greatness. They see no contradiction between their established reputation and the need to advise you of it. They want your obeisance even if they have to teach you what you need to know to supply it. Cigars, this is the culture of cigars, and knowl-edge comes by anecdote. They light their cigars and tell stories from their lives that prove how all the complexities and ambiguities of existence boil down to a few simple lessons that you can learn too if you apply yourself. They are wealthy, having made something that produces income year after year after year without any further effort on their part. They reside in Palm Springs and go regularly to Las Vegas, and to New York every fall to see the new shows. They like Atlantic City, and Chicago, and New Orleans, but wherever they are, they go to the clubs, they visit clubs as other people visit cathedrals, and make a point particularly of going to the small rooms where the new performers are showcasing. They are uneducated men who are proud of their reading and knowledge of human nature. They favor factual work, not fiction, certainly not poetry, but popular military histories and the memoirs of statesmen and inspirational world leaders. From this thin gruel they make a culture by which their minds apprehend the Mysteries. They have written usually hundreds of songs, perhaps two or three or five of which you will recognize as standards, ultimate and lasting artifacts of public consciousness. You will not have to encourage them to sit down at a piano and deliver one of their standards in their usually bad, gravelly voices and incredibly old-fashioned sheet music accompaniment. And they will advise you how many recordings have been made of this song, and by whom, none of them as right in the phrasing, in the interpretation, as their own. They will demonstrate by giving you various readings of crooners and belters and chanteuses, and then showing you how the original, from their throats, is so much better. Tirelessly, exhaustively, they will go through the song again and again, never finding it anything less than fresh though they have been singing it for decades; the song is thirty, forty, fifty years old and is two or three minutes long, and they have been singing it and applauding themselves for it for years, unsated in their wonder for it, the genius of it, that it exists as an achievement as surely as the Capitol in Washington or the four heads of Mount Rushmore. And you wonder— the voice not being there and the music barely, primitively established on the piano, and the words at a level of composition that would make a poet wince or shake his head in pity—how is it the song is so good, so truly fine that recognition surges in you like a current and you laugh for the pleasure of it? How is it from the

vulgar tongue and squawking throat, from the dulled and cat-
aractous eye, from the lobeless brain of this irremediable, dimwit,
something has issued that is actually your own dear and cherished
possession, a memory of yourself, a high moment of your own
imagining, some precipitate of your best and most noble expecta-
tion for your life, when you were young and courageous and held
her in knightly idealization, turning, turning around the room in a
shuffling trance, as the sweet band turned its measures on the
scratchy record, and all your aching, swollen blue desires were
given the name of Romance?

—

The more I think about songs, the more mysterious they become.
They stand in our minds as spiritual histories of certain times; they
have the capacity to represent, in their lyrics and lines of melody,
wars and other disasters, moral process, the fruits of experience,
and, like prayers, the consolations beyond loss. Peoples are brought
into being by them. They are a resource both for the loyalists defending their country and the revolutionists overthrowing it. Yet
they are such short and linear things. Little sale tags on life. Their
rhythms alone can establish states of mind that are imperially pre-
emptive and, by implication, condescending of all other states of
mind. Yet it is essential for their effect that they not go on and on.
Not only their single-mindedness but their brevity makes them universally and instantly accessible as no other form is. To cure up life
into a lyricized tune is to do tremendous violence to reality, and
this is the source of their powerful magic.

—

What happens in a song that differentiates it from speech, even
poetic speech? What makes the spoken voice the singing voice,
when does the pitch of a voice become its note, how does the enu-
meration of a word become the sung word? I've just listened to a
song. Words—the vowels of words—are elongated in songs to such
an extent that if you spoke the lines of a lyric, without its music but

with the vowels held as they are when they are sung, people would not wait to hear the ends of your sentences. This is most particularly true of ballads and love songs, less so of novelty numbers or humorous songs, or songs that take exception to someone's behavior. But it is possible that the appeal of a song lies partly in its deceleration of thought, a release perhaps from the normal race of the mind through its ideas and impressions. To ritually retard a thought is to dwell in its meaning, to find the pleasures of posed conflicts and their resolutions as you would not in a mere recitation of lyrics.

But everyone understands the difference between song and speech, even children, suggesting that the grunt and the note are equally inborn. The question then arises, why is song for the occasion and speech for the everyday? Why do we not sing most of the time, as they do in operas, and speak when we make the especial effort to compact and elevate our feelings?

—

Lullabies, school songs, anthems, battle hymns, work songs, chanteys, love songs, bawdy songs, laments, requiems. They're there in every age of life, for every occasion, on the sepulchral voices of the choir, in the stomp and shout of the whorehouse piano player. But all songs are songs of justification.

—

There are no science songs that I know of. No song that tells you the force of gravity is a product of the masses of two objects divided by the inverse ratio of the distance between them. Science is self-justifying and neither seeks nor offers redress. Yet science teaches us something about song: Scientific formulas describe the laws by which the physical universe operates and suggest in equations that a balance is possible even when things are in apparent imbalance. So do songs. Songs are compensatory. When a singer asks, Why did you do this to me, why did you break my heart?, the inhering formula is that the degree of betrayal is equivalent to the eloquence of the cry of pain. The rage is the square root of love multiplied by a power of the truth of the situation. Feelings transform as quickly and recklessly as subatomic events, and when there is critical mass a song erupts, but the overall amount of pure energy is constant. And when the song is good we recognize it as truth. Like a formula, it applies to everyone, not just the singer.

—

If we sang most of the time, as they do in operas, our lives would resound, as legends; there would be very little room for new data and few occasions to genuinely advance the race, for each small thought or change of direction, each human ploy or representation of feeling, would be monumental. You will notice in classical operas that time moves more slowly than it does before the curtain goes up or after it comes down. There is an actual time warp in every operatic performance between the opening scene of the first act and the closing scene of the last, and that is because the number of narrative events is actually quite small, whereas the reactions to each of them are quite extended. If we sang most of the time, as people do in operas, we would endlessly stand and arrange and rearrange ourselves to offer our solos and the duets and trios and quartets and quintets and choruses of our relationships, and the volatility of the world would diminish, time itself would have to wait for us to register every change of weather with an aria, and we would all move in stately slow motion and rap our staffs upon the earth to bring up the nether spirits, and they would come, because opera is song that has moved outward in all directions and enveloped the entire world in performance, and all the operas ever written are, conglomerately, one song swollen into cosmos.

—

There are publicly held songs whose authorship is anonymous and there are privately held songs that are the copyrighted property of the composer. Folk songs coming out of the hills, up from the mines, fading behind the night train like its whistle. Measuring the time of the long swings of the sledgehammer between bursts of stone. On the one hand. And on the other, what is worked out at the piano, his burning cigarette scoring a black groove in the lid of the upright, the chord bursts interrupted by urgently penciled notations on the staff.

We make distinctions between what is anonymous and known, historic and contemporary, amateur and professional. We make distinctions of motive, or felt reality. The voice that finds words for the pain. The voice that chooses words to convey the pain.

Yet the basic and defining distinction is between an oral culture and a written. Enduring folk songs are standards composed orally and given directly into the air, without notation and, therefore, without regard to property rights. Every song, even a so-called folk song, is composed by one person or perhaps by two. But when the song is not written, the creator of the song has neither the means of protecting it nor the opportunity of seeing to it that it is replicated, as it is, by other performers. Perhaps this is not even conceived as desirable, or more likely not even thought of as a possibility.

Oral cultures are proud, creative, participatory; the mind gives as it receives; and it is not always clear where the self ends and the community begins. So that over the years if the composed but unwritten song endures, it suffers changes, amendments, revisions, refinements, bevelings, planings, sandings, polishings, oilings, rubbings, handlings, until it stands, as elegantly simple in its presence, as glowing in its grain, as a beautiful piece of country cabinetry.

"Come all you fair and tender ladies, take warning how you court young men, they're like a star of the summer morning, they first appear and then they're gone." The gender sorrow of centuries is in those lines. The counsel is worn pure. You remember how from the porch of the dark mansard house along the railroad track she watched from the open door day after day, night after night, and saw in its blinding sunlight or deep violet starlight the terrible unbroken view of the wide but cultivated plains? At dawn the men appeared on the low horizon flinging the sheaves of hay on the wagons trailing the mechanical reaper, which she heard from this distance as the perturbation of bedclothes, a rasp of breath, a soft and toneless grunt of discovery. Well, it goes back beyond the reaper to the scythe, and back beyond the five-string banjo to the lute: You see her? It's the same woman standing there. But she's in the muck yard, walled by the small shire houses of sod and thatch, with only God and her tight linen cap to protect her from the defilation of her lord.

Whereas today songs are written on paper and published and copyrighted. They may be interpreted but not changed. And it is as if the spirit voices in the air have gone silent as God has been silent since we wrote down his words in a book. "Tell me how long the train's been gone," says another old song, and that is what it is talking about.

—

Perhaps the first songs were lullabies. Perhaps mothers were the first singers. Perhaps they learned to soothe their squirming simian babies by imitating the sounds of moving water—the gurgles, cascades, plashes, puddlings, flows, floods, spurts, spills, gushes, laps, and sucks. Perhaps they knew their babies were born from water. And rhythm was the gentle rock of the water hammock slung between the pelvic trees. And melody was the sound the water made when the baby stirred its limbs.

There is the endless delight we take in new beings, the precious fleshlings of our future, our cuntlets and cocklings, our dolls stamped out by God; and there is the antediluvian rage they evoke by their blind, screaming, shitting, and pissing helplessness. So the songs for them are two-faced, lulling in the gentle maternal voice but viciously surrealistic in the words: "Rock-a-bye baby in the treetop, when the wind blows the cradle will rock, when the bough breaks the cradle will fall, down will come baby, cradle and all." Imagine falling through a tree, your legs locked and your arms tightly bound to your sides. Imagine falling down into the world with your little head bongoing against the boughs and the twigs and branches whipping across your ears as if you were a xylophone. Imagine being born. Lullabies urge us to go to sleep at the same time they enact for us the terror of waking. In this way we learn for our own sake the immanence in all feelings of their opposite. The Bible, too, speaks of this as the Fall.

———

"Goober Peas" was a popular song during the Civil War. Goober peas came in a can. They were a ubiquitous field ration. "Peas! Peas! Peas! Peas! Eating goober peas. Goodness how delicious, eating goober peas." This song represents one of the earliest expressions of the irony of ordinary soldiers given to the glory of war. Historians tell us the Civil War was the first instance of modern warfare, by which they mean the moment when the technology of arms became more important than the courage of men. (Yes, if you watch him beheaded in the charge by a shell fired a mile away. Yes, if you have the eyes to watch his body gridded, scored, perforated, and sectioned, quartered, dismembered, and disemboweled with such mechanical efficiency that he is a putrefying blood blob percolating into the earth even as his anguished "Maaa!" still sings in the air.) In recognition of this truth the irony of ordinary soldiers creeps into the campground. We may imagine them marching there singing "The Battle Hymn of the Republic," but in the evening before their action, in contemplation of their death at dawn, when they will run in their chill across the strangely silent meadow, with the familiar beloved scent of hay in their nostrils, and dew loomed in delicate webs of white on the grass, and the woods ahead of them drawn downward by the sunlight, first the treetops and then the slowly thickening trunks, until they see the lead raking toward them as sizzles of light—in contemplation of this they regard one another around the campfire and laugh and sing as raucously as they can, "Peas! Peas! Peas! Peas! Eating goober peas. Goodness how delicious, eating goober peas."

———

"(She's Only) A Bird in a Gilded Cage" is a song written at the turn of the century. The tone of this song is moralistic, compassionately reproachful. A young girl marries an old man for his money and, having done so, dies of lack of love. But popular culture finds its truest expression in the patently moral and covertly lascivious. Think of her drifting through the oppressive rooms of her husband's home—velour drapes, tapestries of the hunt, plush sofas and throne chairs, the thick Persian rugs, the tasseled bellpulls. She wears obsidian bracelets on her arms. Her fingers are ringed and she removes each ring ceremoniously when she sits down to practice the piano. She married money and money keeps even the windows sealed, the cries of the street muted and fading, like her memory. Once she ran free up and down the dank stairwells of poverty, with her cracked ankle shoes slipping off her heels. There was a smart and angry mother upstairs who trained her away from the artless desires and glittering eyes of adoration of the neighborhood boys. There was a father who knew what he had to sell. And now the bird sits and practices her étude, her most taxing physical task of the day. She will be given tea soon, and settled for her afternoon nap, and helped with her bath, and dressed for dinner, and will present herself to her husband at an alluring distance downtable from him. Lonely, pampered, imprisoned in idleness, she will find the one form of expression left to her when at last, in the dark light of her bedroom, with his assistance, she prepares for bed.

"Her beauty was sold for an old man's gold. She's a bird in a gilded cage." If written today, of course, the young woman would not die. The last verse would have her blotting the dribble of oatmeal from the old man's trembling chin and striding off to her classes in medical school. But as a moralistic (if hypocritical) text from the late nineteenth century, the song portrays a common social disaster.

A song written about the same time is "Come Home, Father." The child stands at the bar, pulling on the sleeve of the drunken father. In a sense this is a companion song, a male version of

"(She's Only) A Bird in a Gilded Cage." Both songs describe characteristic recourses of the American working poor in the second half of the nineteenth century.

—

With Tin Pan Alley, songs became a widely distributed industrial spiritual product. The standards that emerged from this manufactory release us into a flow of imagery that whirls us through our decades, our eras, our changing landscape. For a long while industrialized America looks back longingly at its rural past: "When You Were Sweet Sixteen," it sighs, "In the Evening by the Moonlight," "On the Banks of the Wabash," "In the Good Old Summertime." Then the spirit changes; defiance, rebelliousness, is encoded in the sophistications of the double entendre: "(You Can Go as Far as You Like With Me) In My Merry Oldsmobile," "There'll Be a Hot Time (In the Old Town, Tonight)," "It Don't Mean a Thing If It Ain't Got That Swing."

—

When a song is a standard it can reproduce itself from one of its constituent parts. If you merely recite the words you will hear the melody. If you hum the melody the words will articulate themselves in your mind. That is an indication of an unusual self-referential power—the physical equivalent would be regeneration of a severed limb, or cloning an entire being from one cell. Standards from every period of our lives remain cross-indexed in our brains, to be called up in whole, or in part, or, in fact, to come to mind unbidden. Nothing else can as suddenly and poignantly evoke the look, the feel, the smell of our times past. We use standards in the privacy of our minds as signifiers of our actions and relationships. They can be a cheap means of therapeutic self-discovery. If, for example, you are deeply in love and thinking about her and looking forward to seeing her, pay attention to the tune you're humming. Is it "Just One of Those Things"? You will soon end the affair.

—

Of Great Songs, the men who wrote them will tell you the basic principle of composition. Keep it simple. The simpler, the better. You want untrained voices to handle it in the shower, in the kitchen. Try to keep the tune in one octave. Stick with the four basic chords and avoid tricky rhythms. They may not know that this is the aesthetic of the church hymn. They may not know that hymns were the first hits. But they know that hymns and their realm of discourse ennoble or idealize life, express its pieties, and are in themselves totally proper and appropriate for all ears. And so most popular ballads are, in their characteristic romanticism, secularized hymns.

—

The principle of keeping it simple suggests why many standards sound alike. One might even say a song can't become a standard unless it is reminiscent of existing standards. Maybe this is why we feel a new good song has the characteristic of seeming, on first hearing, always to have existed. In a sense it has. Just as we in our own minds seem to have always existed, regardless of the date of our birth, a standard suggests itself as having been around all along, and waiting only for the proper historical moment in which to reveal itself.

When people say "our song" they mean they and the song exist together as some sort of generational truth. They are met to make a common destiny. The song names them, it rescues them from the accident of ahistorical genetic existence. They are located in cultural time. A crucial event, a specific setting, a certain smile, a kind of lingo, a degree of belief or skepticism, a particular humor, or a dance step, goes with the song. And from these ephemera we make our place in civilization. For good or bad, we have our timely place.

—

Today different kinds of songs have different venues. Pop in cafés, show tunes in theaters, rock in stadia, country in roadhouses, bluegrass at outdoor festivals, gospel in churches, evangelical pop on TV networks, blues in clubs. It's a kind of fissioning America we find in our songs. And the music of different singing voices, with different lights in the singers' eyes, ingenious idle musical thoughts, and worked-out ideas of different wisdoms, has all hardened into conventions we call genres. And genres we call markets. Songs come in records, tapes, CDs, videos; come in commercials; come in concerts. Songs on the airwaves pour out one right after another, jammed up, no space between them.

If we allow that culture by its nature imprisons perception, that for a poignant creative moment it may enlighten us but then, perversely, transforms itself into a jailhouse walling out reality, then songs are the cells of our imprisonment. Behind them rise the tiers and guard towers and electrified fences—sitcoms, sermons, movies, newspapers, presidential elections, art galleries, museums, therapies, plays, poems, novels, and university curricula.

But the bars we grasp are our songs.

(1991)

JAMES WRIGHT
AT KENYON

I met James Wright at Kenyon in the dark fall of 1948. If there had been no world war nor the chastened enlightenment that had succeeded it in academic circles, neither of us would have been there. Kenyon had been a kind of club for the sons of wealthy midwestern families. Founded by an Episcopal bishop in 1824 on a hill in central Ohio, it was a handsome school of a character that might best be described as homespun Western Reserve overlaid with Oxonian pretensions. You could read in the architecture of the ivied buildings the devout self-satisfaction of early alumni. There were huge oaks and elms and maples to carve out the generous volumes of space in the college park, and a Middle Path down which the fraternity boys sang every Tuesday evening after dinner as they marched off to perform secret rituals in their lodges in the woods. In the flatlands to the east, just inside the curving single track of a Baltimore and Ohio spur, were the hangars where the collegians of the thirties had kept their biplanes. They also fielded a polo team.

Wright came from poor country people who'd lived for generations on the Ohio River. Only the GI bill made college a possibility for him. He'd served in the army of occupation in Japan, and it was there that another classmate of ours, Jack Furniss, who was serving in the same outfit and was planning to attend Kenyon, had persuaded Wright he might do the same. The selling point was poetry. John Crowe Ransom was on the Kenyon faculty and publishing *The Kenyon Review* from the basement of Ascension Hall.

I too had been drawn to the idea of this small campus at which John Crowe Ransom taught. My high school grades had been erratic but my school, the Bronx High School of Science, was prestigious and Kenyon accepted me. To this day I don't understand how I had known about Ransom, how I as a teenager could have made this knowledgeable choice and found my way to central Ohio. Perhaps my high school guidance counselor saw in my New York folksinging background the makings of a good Southern Agrarian. In any event here I was, age seventeen, as far away from home as I'd ever been. My father had taken a bank loan to pay my tuition. I needed to make the grades for a scholarship. I was reading Milton and Matthew Arnold. It all seemed so sudden. I couldn't easily concentrate.

In fact this classically beautiful campus was in spiritual turmoil. Forces were in contention for it. Naturally this was difficult for a freshman to understand who assumes the entire world to be confidently secured, with only himself in irresolute states of longing and confusion.

The administration's goal to change Kenyon from the second-rate school that it had been was articulated before the war by its new president, Gordon Keith Chalmers, who had pedagogical sympathies with Robert Hutchins at the University of Chicago. It was Chalmers who had brought in Ransom, and his colleague on the *Review*, the philosopher Phillip Blair Rice, as seed for a new, distinguished faculty in the humanities that slowly, duly developed. And the student body was rising to this level: The enlightened postwar admissions policy of the school was to open it up—not only to veterans but to good students from public high schools. None of this came without its costs, however; there was resistance—some of the attitudes and customs of the old school had persisted. But Wright was one of the veterans whose presence on the campus was inevitably challenging the complacent character of the traditional student body, the drinkers and the jocks and the proud C-average second- or third-generation Kenyon men who wore gray flannels and white bucks and school sweaters in the monarchical colors of purple and white. The veterans had brought a nice hard skeptical edge to all of this pretension, and they had a certain authority. They tended to be good students, tough classicists, tough poets, tying into another, slimmer tradition, if it was that, exemplified by the Ransomites of 1940, who had included Robert Lowell and Peter Taylor and their young instructor Randall Jarrell.

But Kenyon now offered its halls to a variety of exotics—Jews and Irish Catholics from New York and Philadelphia, the first two black men ever admitted, foreign students, homosexuals, farmhands, and a fair number of unprepossessing boys given to social afflictions like acne or stuttering. The only thing common to them all was the disposition to do well academically. In fact it was this group, the Independents, as they were called, because for the most part they either could not or did not want to join one of the eight fraternities that ruled the social life of the small college, who were now routinely making the best grades, pulling down all the honors, and graduating into the most prestigious graduate schools.

This was the group to which Wright and I sociologically belonged and to whose standards we aspired. We had met at the Commons. In those days they put out the food at refectory tables and then opened the doors and got out of the way. There was always a stampede, for the table arrangements inevitably reflected our place in the great chain of Kenyon's being. Fraternities sat together, or varsity teams, or people who shared one of the more esoteric majors, like theology, and nobody wanted to be caught with the wrong crowd. I went for the unaffiliated table, of course, where the raucous Independents held court, and that is how, inevitably, one day I found myself sitting next to Wright. He was a hulking fellow, not particularly tall but built like a wrestler, with sloping shoulders and a size eighteen neck. He wore army issue fatigue pants and a sweatshirt; this costume he would vary only, as I learned over time, with a pair of stiff new overalls. He had a round face with particularly small features—small mouth, and small eyes encircled with a pair of colorless plastic GI glasses, which he regularly adjusted because his small nose had not a sufficient bridge to keep them up where they belonged. He spoke in a high but richly timbred voice, like a tenor's. His conversation was intense, opinionated, heavy with four-letter words, but what made it astonishing was that it was interwoven with recitations of poetry. I had never heard anything like it. He would glide from ordinary speech to verse without dropping a beat. It was as if recitation was a normal part of ordinary discourse. Sometimes the lines were appropriate to the subject under discussion, other times not, as if he had been running through them silently in his mind and they just happened to break into his speech, or they had been summoned up from some area of his unconscious and he was merely giving voice to them as a madman speaking to himself. But it all made perfect sense, somehow, and left you awed, because it was a whole system of mind. He knew reams of English poetry from memory and he was helplessly engaged with it. We sat long after the meal was over. He drank coffee and smoked a cigarette, holding it in a peculiarly European way, between the third and fourth fingers of his hand.

I told him about a discussion in my philosophy class. At this time the national presidential campaign was under way between Harry Truman and Thomas Dewey. Most of the class was for Dewey, the Republican. A couple were for Truman. I thought of the late Franklin Roosevelt as the real president and so was rooting for his one-time vice president Henry A. Wallace, an idealist running on a third-party ticket with leftist backing and getting his comsymp head handed to him. The class had for its text Plato's *Republic*. We'd been meeting in the basement of the college chapel, the Church of the Holy Spirit. When I spoke for Wallace, everyone in the class looked at me—one of those!—and I told Wright it was at that moment I realized what Plato meant by the cave of shadows. He laughed. Then he said in a low growl, suddenly angry, despairing, that Harry Truman had dropped the bomb not once but twice, which made him a son of a bitch for all eternity, that Dewey was a complacent blockhead, and that Henry Wallace was the only one of any of them worth anything as a human being and that was why he was being crucified.

Then all at once he was chanting some lines from Spenser and he asked me if I didn't think they were the most goddamn beautiful lines ever written.

—

That was a cold, beautiful autumn and it grew dark earlier every afternoon. I struggled with my new life. Truman was asking all government employees to sign loyalty oaths. Am I wrong or was Kenyon asking its seventeen-year-old freshmen to do the same thing? Why was there compulsory chapel every Sunday morning? And why were freshmen required to wear beanies? This was 1948, there had been the Holocaust and a world war that had killed forty million people, and the same college that published *The Kenyon Review* expected me to go around with some stupid-ass school cap on my head like an idiot in a Cruickshank drawing. I took my beanie—beanie! the very word in one's mouth was a humiliation—and stuffed it in a garbage can.

What I admired about my new friend Wright was his invulnerability or obliviousness to such struggles. Somehow it had to do with the fact that he was a poet, which is to say he operated at a depth of feeling originating solely within himself. I sought him out whenever I had the chance. He was the first poet I'd ever met. I had known students who wrote verse, of course; I had written some myself. But it seemed to me now that what defined a poet was that he didn't stop being a poet between poems. Poetry was not something one practiced but a state of being in which every moment of one's existence was amplified. You could not be in Wright's presence for five minutes without understanding what it took to get a true line down on a page—what it had taken Edwin Arlington Robinson, for example, or Frost, or Keats, for that matter. It was an intensity of self-generated perception, a raging, all-consuming subjection to your own consciousness, a kind of helplessness, finally.

Wright always carried with him the verses he was working on, in stiff black clamp binders, three or four of them under his arm along with his books. He was never without his work. He seemed to have hundreds of verses and to be subjecting all of them to reconsideration all the time. You'd find him at the Village Inn, sitting alone with a cigarette and a cup of coffee, or in front of a beer at Jean Valjean's, and he'd be hunched in a booth revising a typed draft in his round, grade-school hand.

We did not share any classes. He was a semester or so ahead of me and already at the point of doing only electives. He was taking five or six courses rather than the usual four, not only because he needed to graduate before his GI benefits ran out, but because he had an enormous appetite for literature. He was a prodigious student. He was learning Anglo-Saxon, German, and French. And a language was not just something to take an exam in, it was a music you heard. He discovered in the library a collection of 78s of Elisabeth Schwarzkopf renditions of Schubert lieder; he became a Schwarzkopf addict, listening by the hour. He would emerge from the library and stride down the Middle Path. *Du holde Kunst,* he would sing, *in wieviel grauen Stunden, / Wo mich des Lebens wilder Kreis umstrickt, / Hast du mein Herz zu warmer Lieb entzunden, / Hast mich in eine bessre Welt entrückt!,* this farm boy from Martins Ferry, Ohio, rolling along in his wrestler's gait. He was not susceptible to ordinary judgments.

As the year went on, I found a collegial stance that suited me—or perhaps it was a sense of myself in my generation: I was wary not only of the school's Anglophilic customs but of life itself. There was a war now in Korea I supposed I'd end up in. I became one of those who could read or play ball or drink beer or shoot pool or go into the nearby town of Mt. Vernon to find girls or even study, dispensing to each thing a careless measure of sincerity. Life, whatever that was, was ahead of me—as it was for all of us. There was a kind of metaphysical suspense in our collegiate lives. But Wright seemed beyond that. He seemed to be fully realized for what he was. He had no degrees of sincerity. There was nothing provisional about him. He was the sole, whole, inevitable Jim in every situation, formal or informal, alone or in a crowd, the same helpless poet in all events.

———

In February of 1949 the oldest of the three dormitories, Old Kenyon, burned to the ground one Saturday night just a week before I was to move into a room there. The worst of the fire had occurred in Middle Kenyon, the section of the old building reserved for the unaffiliated students, who had been housed there to make a kind of fraternity in spite of themselves. Nine students were missing, all of them from this group. Like Wright I had been living in temporary barracks the college had set up in the adjoining village of Gambier to accommodate the swollen postwar enrollment. On Sunday morning I went down to the campus and stood looking at the gutted building. You could see the sky through the windows. A mist of blue smoke rose from the ruins. It was very cold, very quiet. Nobody seemed able to move. We heard that the dean of men, Frank Bailey, had rescued several students and was himself in the hospital. At noon the president of the college, Gordon Chalmers, convened everyone at the Commons and called the roll for the entire student body. When someone did not answer to his name, Chalmers asked for friends and acquaintances to stand and try to recall when they had seen him last, in the hope that he had left campus for the weekend. The exercise was futile. Seven of the nine dead students were Jewish. One was Hispanic-Indian.

What was so terrible was not that anyone had deliberately started the fire—that had not been the case—but that it had nevertheless struck so as to reveal to us all how awfully the college still mirrored the society at large.

Students who'd been made homeless doubled up in the other dorms. Students returned from the hospital wearing casts on their arms, or with bandaged heads. Dean Bailey resumed his duties on crutches. The following fall, with Old Kenyon being rebuilt stone for stone, I moved in with the de facto fraternity of Independent survivors now situated in the shingled Alumni House in the village of Gambier at the edge of the college park. It was a raucous year, all of us living in such close quarters in tiny guest rooms. Wright was one of us but he could not afford to live there. From his arrival at Kenyon, he had lived apart even from the people who lived apart— he simply would not be hostage to the frenzies of dormitory life. We invented all manner of games—roof ball, mailbox ball; we redesigned for the front porch city sidewalk games from our childhoods, like boxball; we played three-dimensional tic-tac-toe, bridge; we ran intricate touch football games, or Frisbee pie-plate Olympics; and on rainy days we argued philosophy and literature as if arguing were a sport. I think we were making an alternate college. It was as if the lines had been drawn; some sort of battle for Kenyon's soul was under way, or for our own, although no one would have thought this was the case. The boys who had been most severely injured or closest to the nine who had died were the most antic of all.

So it was a somehow transformed school in my sophomore year. I think of the whole year as a kind of spring, the trees in constant leaf, and a soft, sweet breeze smelling of haymows coming up from the central Ohio farms. It was now apparent that Wright had become for many of us a kind of older brother; he aroused an almost universal respect that was unheard-of in our critical society. There were actually several fine undergraduate poets in residence—Robert Mezey was one—but Wright was their model, central to them all. He had had some verses accepted for publication in *The Kenyon Review.* For an undergraduate poet, that was akin to a Nobel Prize. He roomed off-campus in the home of Professor Timberlake, with whom he was reading *Beowulf.* He was the kind of student with whom a professor would associate. Later he would stay with the family of Professor Hanfman, his German teacher. He was absorbing everything he could of European language, art, music, but without giving up an iota of his midwestern self. He sang lieder, but he loved bawdy army songs too, and one in particular, "Sam, Sam, the Shithouse Man," he taught to several of his entourage so that they made an entire chorus going their satirical way down the Middle Path.

Now I will speak of this entourage, because it is essential to an understanding of Wright at Kenyon. Something had happened, some shift had occurred in the local Zeitgeist—a favorite word of ours—some apolitical assertiveness had arisen that had not been there before the fire, a tiny countercultural blaze of its own burning, probably without our awareness. In James Wright's case this was a new sociability of a very specific kind—the cultivation and celebration of the outcasts and pariahs of the college.

Of course he had always been a great audience for collegiate nonsense. Our witty classmate Billy Goldhurst, for example, did very funny imitations of Bogart and Cagney and liked at odd and inappropriate moments to perform scenes from films from the past —as for instance Raymond Massey's rendition of Lincoln's Gettysburg Address, while we stood behind him and hummed "The Battle Hymn of the Republic," louder and louder, of course, until he had to shout the lines to be heard above our singing. Wright loved this sort of thing. He remembered gags, jokes you had told, lines you came up with, and quoted them back to you weeks later. He broadcast them around the campus. He relished the imitations we did of our teachers—"Pappy" Ransom's soft Virginia dialect, for example, or the way Phil Rice mumbled his incredible lectures while picking shreds of cigarette paper off his lower lip, or the fey lisp of the elderly, somewhat rotund French scholar known to us as "Fauncy," or the almost salivating delivery of one of the European history professors when he came around to his famous lecture on the anatomical peculiarities of Elizabeth I.

Of course students have always irreverently celebrated their professors among themselves. What was noteworthy was the audience Wright made himself for this kind of horseplay. Because he took such appreciative and not particularly discriminating enjoyment from every stupid routine we came up with, we fell into the habit of performing for him and acting like clowns whenever he was around.

I know I felt this tendency within myself. I was not a college poet, I had found new loyalties outside the English department—in the theater and in philosophy—and so perhaps had a sharper sense of the poetry scene at Kenyon than I might have had as an insider. Besides the genuine poets such as Wright and Mezey, there were several poetasters, pretenders who had none of the talent but all of the requisite sensibility, and I remember having my fun one day, consciously going for the laugh, walking with Wright and some other friends in the late autumn, when I suddenly rushed into a pile of raked leaves and kicked them into a cloud and stood in this rain of leaves and raised one limp-wristed hand and said with the tremulous delivery of Blather Bunthorne in *Patience,* "Look, look, the leaves are falling!" And of course, for weeks afterwards that was Jim's greeting to me: "Look, look, the leaves are falling!," followed by his brassy laughter. He never forgot a thing. He had a library of quotes from us all—as subject to the recall of his prodigious memory as any verse in English, from *Piers Plowman* to Robert Service.

Inevitably, in his role as a patron of humor and irreverence, Wright began to attract the weirder students of the community. By our junior year he was associating almost exclusively with the social pariahs, the great offenses to collegiate style and decorum, as rowdy as they may have been. And these were either Middle Kenyon Independents, from the despised of that elegant, outcast group, or campus loners like himself—eccentrics, boys with odd gifts, like tendentiousness, or an encyclopedic knowledge of inconsequential things. They might be students who were physically filthy, and whose eyeglasses were encrusted with dirt; or con men, the shadowy few who seemed to be living at Kenyon with no visible connection at all to academic studies; or fantasists and drunks; or the very shy—he loved the very shy. He loved them all, and I would see him walking down Middle Path while swirling around him, performing without question, was one or more of this repertory company of clowns that he had gathered to himself. He was their audience, laughing uproariously at their antics, bringing them into flower, giving them courage or at least some sense of having, from his recognition of them, a place in the college community.

So that was the entourage. Of course I was by this time not entirely in sympathy with the whole idea. I wondered what Wright was up to. If there was a political dimension to it all, it escaped me. Some of the more outlandish of these boys were simply fools; there was no other word for them. They were just not as funny as he made them out to be. When they were with Jim, I tended to avoid him—go the other way when I saw them all coming. I felt, possibly to my discredit, that he might be unconsciously patronizing them, that apart from his genuine preference for their company, he might be finding a kind of sustenance from it, not entirely to his honor.

There were all sorts of reasons, even at a school as small as Kenyon, for friends to lose close touch with each other. I had in my junior year moved to the heart of the campus in the reconstructed Old Kenyon, fireproofed now with tiled floors and painted cement-block stairwells. I was a full-fledged, intensely serious philosophy major, studying alternately with the members of the best two-man philosophy department in the country, Phil Rice and Virgil Aldrich. A star school actor and veteran, Paul Newman, had gone on to Yale Drama School, and so I found myself landing some good roles in the Drama Club productions—Joe Bonaparte, in Odets's *Golden Boy*, for example. Theater took up an immense amount of time, as did an affair I fell into for a while with a young woman from out of town who had come to act in one of the campus productions. And so I was in my own way living the collegiate life; I was making Kenyon mine with as many claims to my school as the most traditional fraternity boy, establishing myself as each of us had to do, undergoing the crucial, assertive process of self-definition in a constant stream of ideas and feelings.

In the world outside, what were called "atomic spies" were being arrested every week, and the ominous ideology of the cold war had achieved national consensus. *Time* magazine was calling those of us in school the silent generation, which should have been some indication to me that something was already in dissent born—that some small secret transmigration of the nation's soul had been effected and was waiting to reveal itself. Meanwhile I did not entirely appreciate Wright's perhaps most bizarre follower, a fellow named Frank LeFever. I will describe him in his apotheosis, and it will become apparent how prophecy eludes even those most receptive to it. LeFever wore shredded blue jeans cut off at the knees in the warmer weather, and T-shirts with great looping holes and hanging flaps. He never bothered to have his hair cut, so that it hung long and shaggy down the back of his neck. His facial hair too was untended, so that he looked rather oriental, with a wispy brown beard and mustache. I believe he favored workshoes without socks and sometimes affected a single earring, like a Portuguese fisherman. I had no idea what his academic credentials were, but he was Wright's constant companion and lived to entertain him. It was LeFever who stood up at a reading by Robert Frost in Rosse Hall and in front of the whole college shouted, "Mr. Frost, was that a real poem, or did you just make it up?" A nimble fellow, he liked to climb up on the roof of Old Kenyon at night and lope like Quasimodo along the ridge and howl at the moon. All this was a cause of great merriment to the now small company of two or three hardcore rebels who followed James Wright wherever he went. LeFever had a reedy voice that gave sly implications to whatever he said, even in the rare moments when he was serious. But for the most part he knew no restraint. He was disposed to indiscriminate mockery, whether the target was appropriate or not, and so was barely tolerated by most of us as a perpetual adolescent, a kid who didn't know when to stop. But Wright encouraged every alienated impulse it was in LeFever to express and was his sponsor and patron in this time I speak of, 1951, a good dozen years before the dropout spirit as well as the self-display of hair and dress of the hippie movement took hold and became a countercultural phenomenon of the 1960s.

I don't claim prescience for the poet. The political character of this esoteric fraternity of his founding probably escaped him, as it did me. But he was their audience and urgent friend, and they all laughed a lot. He brought out the glories of their incongruous presence on campus and made a culture of their displacement, and with his brassy laughter and academic prowess was a shield for them all. More to the point was the necessity to him of their friendship—I see that in retrospect. It is odd, I suppose, when speaking of a poet, to suggest that there were times when he relied on somebody else to express what he had to say, but I believe it to be so; another voice was required, as in blasphemous counterpoint, some sort of anti-poetry being called for, some vulgar carelessness of all ambition and achievement, including, or especially, his own.

That inner entourage are today rather impressive members of society—of course. LeFever is a well-regarded neuropsychologist in New York. Another, Dr. Eugene Pugatch, is an eminent neurologist —and so on. There is in their example some possibility that the wildest excesses of youthful spirit are truly in service to the ideals of the culture. Not that the Kenyon administration believed this: a year or two after the last of the veterans had gone through, and by the mid-fifties, when Ransom was on the verge of retirement and Phillip Rice had been killed in an automobile accident, those of the irrepressible cadre of Wright's old pals who still were in school were strongly encouraged to leave. And within a few years the right wing at Kenyon had regained its position and admissions policies began to go back to what they had been before the days of Ransom.

—

Not until my senior year would I finally see the root source of James Wright's life and work and begin to understand the immensity of his effort. He invited me to Martins Ferry one cold winter weekend. We hitched a ride into Mt. Vernon and caught a bus that made its circuitous way southeast along two-lane roads, where people waited with their valises at the crossings, and horses stood in the snowfields beside bales of hay. Wright's sole living relative in

Martins Ferry was an aunt. She was a gracious and very humble woman, clearly made uncomfortable by the collegiate ambience we brought with us. The house was quite small, a worker's one-story cottage in a street of them. Our sleeping arrangements consisted of the parlor floor beside the wood stove, with newspapers for blankets. In the morning we went to a diner for breakfast and then crossed the river into Wheeling, West Virginia, where we attended an afternoon concert of the Wheeling Symphony Orchestra, sitting for a dollar each in the almost empty wooden balcony of a hall where there seemed to be more people playing on stage than listening in the audience. It was not an event I would have chosen for myself—the child of music-loving parents in New York who had made him a familiar of Carnegie Hall and the Metropolitan Opera House. But I was incredibly moved. How hard these people played, and how they struggled to do well, and how well they did, and what a profound isolation it was to long for beauty and grace in the industrial heartland of the United States.

Wright at Kenyon had to struggle to make it his. He was carrying within himself such enormous contradictions—this dirt-poor Ohioan set down in the intellectual park of a historic private college, this poet alive in the constitution of a football lineman, this irremediably midwestern American in unslakeable thirst for the language and culture of Europe. Despite his academic successes he was an embattled student. He had the greatest respect for Ransom, of course; possibly he revered him. I have no way of knowing, but I assume he showed a lot of his work to the older poet and received the benefit of Ransom's just and serenely disinterested critical taste. But I cannot imagine that the relationship was close or that it was comfortable for either of them. They were too different as poets and as men. It is my impression that in the year Robert Hillyer served as a visiting professor of English, Wright seemed in his nature to prefer this less fashionable and more romantic poet—at least as a teacher or as a person with whom he could talk.

The Martins Ferry boy was never happy with the New Criticism —something the rest of us practiced at Kenyon the way at Ohio

State they played football. (I remember my sense of achievement when I produced a fifteen-page paper on the eight lines of Wordsworth's "A Slumber Did My Spirit Seal.") As a poet he felt a simple, instinctive aversion to the precisions of textual analysis and the culture of possibly self-satisfied intellectualism that it represented. But as a student he would need to lend himself to the dominating ideals of scrupulous critical speech, the way of talking about the poem that gave it its just due apart from who had written it and when it had been written and what aesthetic/historical principles it gave evidence of. So here was another conflict that had to be accommodated on a constant, daily basis, almost as one would have to deal with physical impairment. I reiterate that Wright had no levels of response other than disproportionate. Once he submitted a poem to the school newspaper, *The Collegian*. After it was accepted and put in type, he decided he didn't like the poem after all and did not want to "stand by it," as he told the paper's editor. I happened to be present at the time. He wanted the poem pulled. The editor refused, saying it was too late, and in any event he, Wright, might be the poet, but not necessarily the best judge of the poem's quality. Wright roared and leaped across the desk. I had to grab his arms and pin them back to keep him from killing the poor pale editor, a thin fellow who walked with a slight limp, as it happened. I shouted for the editor to get the hell out of there, which he hastened to do—I couldn't have held Wright much longer; he was as strong as an ox. Afterwards, when I tried to calm him down, I found that, for my trouble, I had now been associated with an unforgivable affront. My friend would not talk to me for several weeks.

And he was as often as not in some, unfair to him, combat with a teacher. He came to Kenyon already well read, but he went through books almost as though there existed within him a panic that could be stilled only by more and more reading. As an older student, a veteran, he assumed an adult status that his teachers were happy to endorse; at the same time it raised their expectations of him. I remember this characteristic problem came to a head on the occasion of his senior thesis, which turned out to be a 385-page book on Thomas Hardy. Despite its size and its ambition, and the fact that he'd done something truly colossal for an undergraduate, the manuscript was found wanting and returned to him for revision. Wright's reaction to this verged on the suicidal. He did end up reworking the thesis and it was accepted in its revised form, but the experience remained shattering to him—some sort of institutional rebuke to his pride, his appetite for literature, his capacity for work, his claim of a place at the High Table for James Wright of Martins Ferry, Ohio.

—

Here this little memoir of Wright at Kenyon properly ends. We were graduated in the same class, 1952, though he had in fact finished all his requirements a semester earlier. My memory picks him up a few months later in New York, where he stopped en route to his Fulbright in Vienna. He was with his new wife, Liberty. A few of us were boarding in a railroad flat on West Ninety-second Street that was the home of the Goldhurst brothers, Richard and Billy, both of Kenyon—the same apartment where some years before, Allen Ginsberg and Jack Kerouac used to hang out. James Wright was on his way to Europe in his old army lace-up boots and fatigues and a jacket too small for his bulk. He held the inevitable cigarette between the wrong fingers and carried his hard black notebooks filled with new poems. He read to us in his tenor voice; I think he actually trained his voice to a lower pitch as he moved on in his career as a reader of poetry. He left an extra pair of shoes behind, which he then petitioned us to mail to him, and we eventually did, but not soon enough to be kind. Thereafter I saw him less and less frequently, I am terribly sad to say. I followed his publications with immense pride, but no astonishment. All of us at Kenyon had known he was the real thing. But I did regret it when in my view he seemed to be sucked into the tiny swamp of professional poetry in the United States. The poets in all their flailing intensity could really keep each other gasping. I did see at this or that read-

ing the continuous attraction he had for loyal followers, for an entourage. But by then I understood the necessity for it, and
American poetry's awful surrounding silence.

One evening years ago, James Wright came to visit me in New
Rochelle, where I had settled with my wife and children. He stayed
overnight and did not sleep well—we heard him cry out from time
to time. But in the morning I found him sitting at the breakfast table
reciting poems to my three children. He sat in his boots and trousers and ribbed undershirt with a glass of bourbon in front of him
and a cigarette in his hand, and because my elder daughter's name
is Jenny, he gave us "Jenny Kissed Me." And while these three little
children stared at him and slowly chewed their cornflakes, he went
from Sidney to Donne to Pope to Thomas Gray, and while my wife
in her bathrobe was making their peanut butter sandwiches for
their lunch bags, he came up in history through Browning and
Tennyson, and eventually got to the German poet, Trakl, and re-
cited, as I blinked and drank my coffee, a poem about German
decadence, and it was not yet eight o'clock in the morning.

The last time I saw my friend he was in Mt. Sinai hospital in New
York, terribly ill, terminally ill, and he could no longer speak. He
had a grommet in his throat to maintain the tracheotomy that
would allow him to breathe. His mouth was packed with some sort
of medicinal batting. He had been remarried for many years to
Anne Wright. She was there with him and handed him a clipboard
with a pad. He wrote something and handed it to me. I could feel
his eyes as he watched my face for my reaction. I read in the same
round grade-school hand I remembered: "The leaves are falling."

(1990)

Two Waldens

Thoreau's *Walden; or, Life in the Woods*, like Twain's *Huckleberry Finn*, or Melville's *Moby-Dick*, is a book that could only have been written by an American. You can't imagine this odd, visionary, but very tough work coming out of Europe. It is peculiarly of us; it is indelibly made from our woods and water and New World ethos. But more than that, it is one of the handful of works that make us who we are. *Walden* is crucial to the identity of Americans who have never read it and have barely heard of Thoreau. Its profound complaint endures to our century—for example, it was the text of choice in the 1960s, when the desire to own nothing and live poor swept through an entire generation.

It is a sometimes prickly book about independence, and a practical how-to book on the way to live close to the earth in a self-sufficient manner; it is a sometimes philosophical book about values—what we need to live in self-realization and what we don't need, what is true and important, what is false and disabling; and it is a religious book about being truly awake and alive in freedom in the natural world and living in a powerful transcendent state of reverence toward it. *Walden* is all of these together. Presented as the story of Thoreau's life at the pond over a period of two years, it fuses his political, economic, social, and spiritual ideas in a vision of supreme common sense.

All right, that begins to describe the book. What about the place? We have the book—why do we need the place?

Literature, like history, endows places with meaning, locates them in the moral universe, gives them a charged name. So in effect literature connects the visible and the invisible. It finds the meaning, or the hidden life, in the observable life. It discovers the significant secrets of places and things. That is what makes it so necessary to us; that is why we practice it; that is why it is such an essential human function. Uncharged with invisible meaning, the visible is nothing, mere clay; and without a visible circumstance, a territory, to connect to, our spirit is shapeless, nameless, and undefined.

"Near the end of March, 1845," Thoreau writes, "I borrowed an axe and went down to the woods by Walden Pond nearest to where I intended to build my house, and began to cut down some tall arrowy white pines. . . ." Walden is the material out of which Thoreau made his book—as surely as he made his house from the trees he cut there, he made his book from the life he lived there. The pond and woods are the visible, actual, real source of Thoreau's discovered, invisible truths, the material from which he made not only his house but his revelation.

That Walden is a humble place—an ordinary pond, a plain New England wood—is exactly the point. Thoreau made himself an Everyman, and chose Walden for his Everywhere.

Clearly there is a historical luminosity to these woods. They stand transformed by Thoreau's attention into a kind of chapel in which this stubborn Yankee holy man came to his and, as it turns out, our redemptive vision. So there is a crucial connection of American clay and spirit here: If we neglect or deface or degrade Walden, the place, we sever a connection to ourselves, we tear it asunder. Destroy the place and we defame the author, mock his vision, and therefore tear up by the root the spiritual secret he found for us.

We need both Waldens, the book and the place. We're not all spirit any more than we are all clay; we are both and so we need both—as in: You've read the book, now see the place.

You have to be able to take the children there, and to say "This is it, this is the wood Henry wrote about. You see?" You give them what is rightfully theirs, just as you give them Gettysburg because it is theirs.

But in fact you don't even have to see the place as long as you know it's there and it looks much as it looked when he was cutting the young white pines for his house. Then it is truly meaningful in spirit and in clay—like us, and like the world invisibly charged with our idea of it.

And so for these reasons, to defend a masterwork from desecration and ourselves from self-mutilation, I stand with this group of citizens who declare here, today, that Walden Woods will be returned to its natural state.

(1990)

Notes

"Standards" is the only piece in this book that was not commissioned. It was published in *Harper's* in 1991.

"Jack London and His Call of the Wild" combines a review of the three-volume edition of his *Letters* and of *American Dreamers* by Clarice Stasz, published in *The New York Times Book Review* in 1989, with the introduction to the Vintage Library of America edition of *The Call of the Wild*, published in 1990.

"Theodore Dreiser: Book One" was written as the introduction for the Bantam Classics edition of *Sister Carrie*, published in 1982. "Book Two" was originally a review of Dreiser's second, incomplete, and only recently published work, *An Amateur Laborer*, and appeared in *The New York Times Book Review* in 1983.

"Ernest Hemingway, R.I.P.," a review of the posthumous and heavily edited novel *The Garden of Eden*, was first published in *The New York Times Book Review* in 1983.

"Orwell's *1984*" was published anticipatorily in 1983, in different form, by *Playboy* magazine.

"Ronald Reagan" was written for *The Nation* in 1980.

"Commencement," an address given to the graduating class of 1989 at Brandeis University, was published later the same year in *The Nation*.

"The Character of Presidents" was originally published in *The Nation* during the election campaign of 1992.

"The Beliefs of Writers" was the Hopwood Lecture delivered to graduating students of the Creative Writing Program at the University of Michigan in 1984; it was published in 1985 in *The Michigan Quarterly Review*. (An abridged version appeared in *The New York Times Book Review* under the title "The Passion of Their Calling.")

"A Citizen Reads the Constitution" was originally an address given at Constitution Hall in Philadelphia in 1986 under the auspices of the Pennsylvania Humanities Council. It was published by *The Nation* in 1987.

"The Nineteenth New York" was originally published in *Architectural Digest* in 1992.

"False Documents" was first published in slightly different form in *New American Review* (Bantam), 1977.

"James Wright at Kenyon" appeared in the *Gettysburg Review* in 1990.

"Two Waldens" consists of remarks made at the Walden Woods Project Press Conference held in Boston, Massachusetts, on April 25, 1990. This conference inititiated a citizens' effort to purchase Walden Woods from private developers and preserve it for posterity.

E. L. DOCTOROW is the author of *Welcome to Hard Times* (1960), *Big as Life* (1966), *The Book of Daniel* (1971), *Ragtime* (1975), *Loon Lake* (1980), *Lives of the Poets* (1984), *World's Fair* (1985), and *Billy Bathgate* (1989). His play, *Drinks Before Dinner* (1978), was produced by the New York Shakespeare Festival. Mr. Doctorow is the recipient of the National Book Critics Circle Award, the National Book Award, the John Simon Guggenheim Fellowship, and the Arts and Letters award and the William Dean Howells medal of the American Academy of Arts and Letters. He is Glucksman Professor of American and English Letters at New York University.

ABOUT THE TYPE

The text of this book was set in Palatino, designed by the German typographer Hermann Zapf. It was named after the Renaissance calligrapher Giovanbattista Palatino. Zapf designed it between 1948 and 1952, and it was his first typeface to be introduced in America. It is a face of unusual elegance.